IMAGES of ENGLAND

STOCKPORT
REVISITED

THE OLD WHITE LION

ST PETERSGATE

LOWER HILLGATE

Stockport

HILLGATE

EDGELEY ROAD

IMAGES OF ENGLAND

STOCKPORT
REVISITED

MORRIS GARRATT

TEMPUS

Frontispiece: Postcard with six views of Stockport.

First published 2006

Tempus Publishing Limited
The Mill, Brimscombe Port,
Stroud, Gloucestershire, GL5 2QG
www.tempus-publishing.com

© Morris Garratt, 2006

The right of Morris Garratt to be identified as the Author
of this work has been asserted in accordance with the
Copyrights, Designs and Patents Act 1988.

All rights reserved. No part of this book may be reprinted
or reproduced or utilised in any form or by any electronic,
mechanical or other means, now known or hereafter invented,
including photocopying and recording, or in any information
storage or retrieval system, without the permission in writing
from the Publishers.

British Library Cataloguing in Publication Data.
A catalogue record for this book is available from the British Library.

ISBN 0 7524 4172 8

Typesetting and origination by Tempus Publishing Limited.
Printed in Great Britain.

Contents

	Acknowledgements	6
	Introduction	7
one	The 'Old' Stockport	9
two	School Days	37
three	Hatting, Brewing and Other Industries	47
four	Moving Around	63
five	The Heatons	77
six	The 'New' Stockport	89
seven	The Williams Family	109
eight	And Finally…	125

Acknowledgements

As before, I am deeply indebted to many organisations and individuals who have given me access to their collections and have placed photographs in their possession at my disposal. My first debt must be to the Executive Committee of the Stockport Historical Society for granting me access to the extensive collections of slides made and archived by various past and present members of the Society; without this the compilation of the present book would have been much more difficult. I am also pleased to record my thanks to: Mr David Reid and the ever-helpful staff of the Local Heritage Library; Stockport Central Library, for their assistance and knowledge once again so freely given; staff at 'Hatworks' (Stockport Hat Museum) and Luton Museum; Mrs Linda Lewis, formerly of Edgeley but now in Australia, who, when she knew a second book was being contemplated, immediately offered items from her personal archive; Mrs Enid Price and Mr John Price; Mrs Shirley McKenna, who unfortunately could not join me again for the compilation of this volume; the un-named photographers of the local newspapers, both past and present; Miss Dorothy Westhead; Miss Sheila Crossley; Mr Roy Westall; Miss Madelaine Wagstaff; Mrs Pat and Mr Philip Rigley; Mr Peter Needham; Mrs Eileen Garratt; Mrs Jennifer Garratt; Mrs Sue Hill, of Chatham, Kent; Mrs Jill Gourley; Mr David Huxley and Mr Neil McAllister.

For the verification of facts my indebtedness to previously published books on Stockport and the individual townships will be obvious, but may I nevertheless thank Dr Peter Arrowsmith, Mrs Heather Coutie, Mr Ray Preston, Mrs Ann Hearle, and the members of the Heatons Research Group, Stockport Historical Society for their valuable contributions to the history of both the 'old' and the 'new' Stockport.

I have made every effort to obtain the permission of copyright owners to reproduce these images and I apologise if I have inadvertently offended anyone's rights. In such cases, please contact me via the publisher's address and I will rectify any errors in any subsequent reprints of this book.

Morris Garratt
July 2006

Introduction

When the first book on Stockport in this series was published in 1999 the compilers wondered whether the local market for books of this kind was now satisfied, but we have been proved wrong! The success of that first book resulted in a request for a second one, and this is it! That first one concentrated on the area of the former county borough, so in this one I have taken the opportunity to broaden the scope of the book by including images from some of the areas now incorporated within the enlarged Stockport Metropolitan Borough as a result of the Local Government Act 1974. It has often been remarked that 'even yesterday is history', and while none of the photographs are quite that recent, there are a number dating from the 1960s and later, which in historical terms is 'yesterday'!

In 1844 Friedrich Engels described Stockport as 'one of the darkest and smokiest holes in the whole industrial area'. Looking at the forest of mills and chimneys in this print from 1885, it is not difficult to see why!

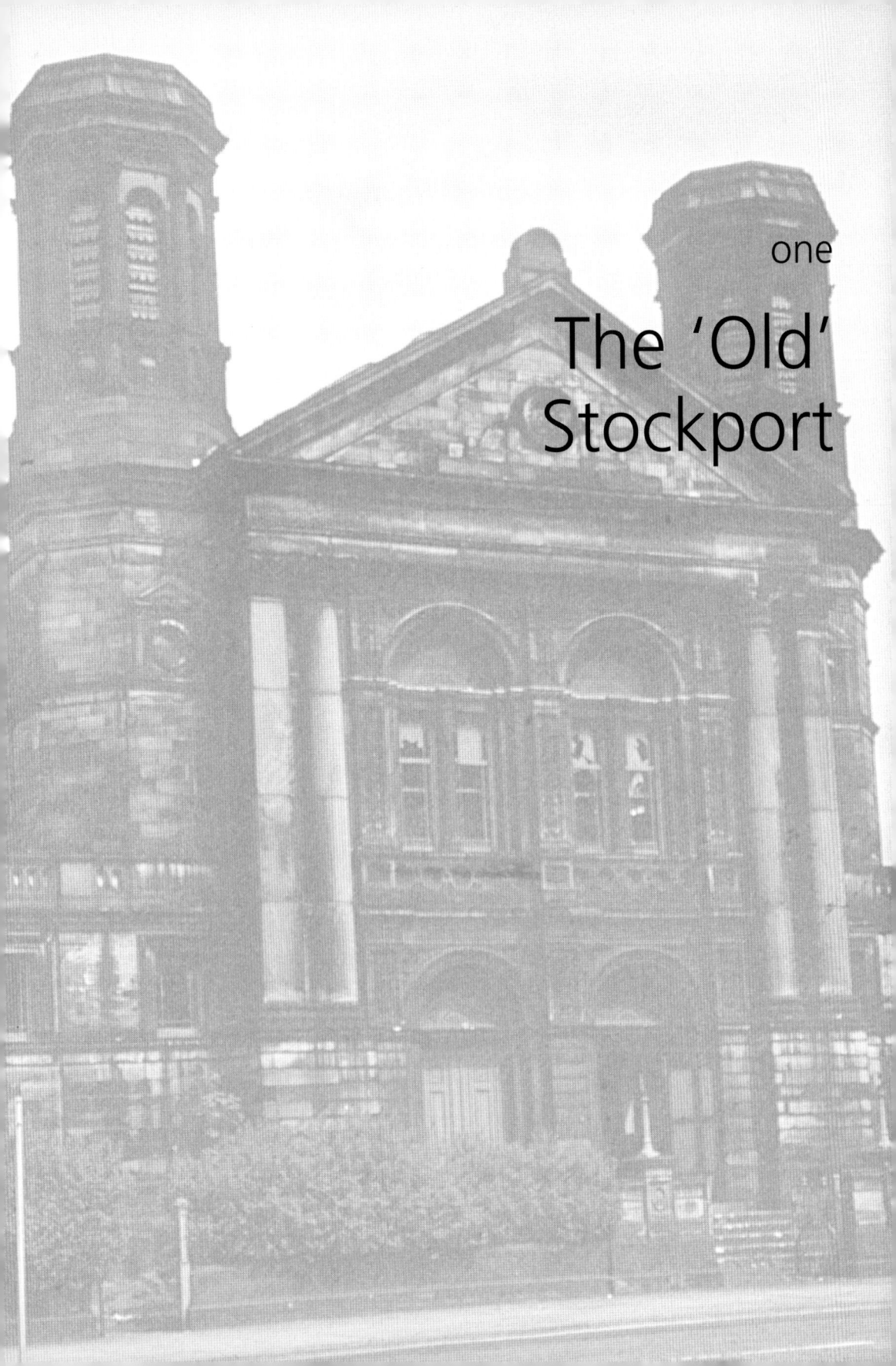

one

The 'Old' Stockport

Stockport Town Hall, built to the design of Sir Alfred Brumwell Thomas, was opened on 7 July 1908. The foundation stone was laid by the Mayor, Alderman Giles Atherton, a local brewer, on 15 October 1904. Here the Royal carriage with the Prince and Princess of Wales (later King George V and Queen Mary) enters Prince's Street on its way to the opening ceremony.

The top stone, almost a ton in weight, was set in place on 30 January 1907.

Workmen building the Town Hall.

The Maia Choirs were founded by Thomas Kay in 1903. The Town Hall is the setting for this picture taken on 17 February 1939.

Here the choir is seen carol singing outside Stockport Infirmary, c. 1934.

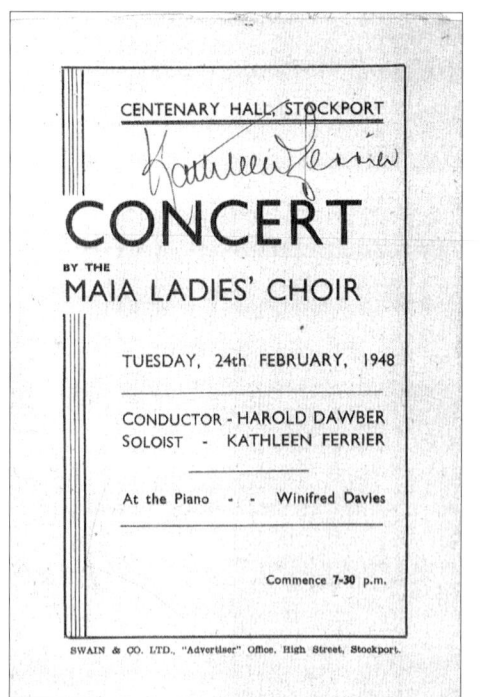 

Above: The choir's soloists were eminent singers of the day and here are two autographed programmes.

Below: The present appearance of the choir stalls of Stockport parish church, seen here in an early postcard, results from its rebuilding in 1813-17; the only survival from the previous medieval church is the chancel, built in the Decorated style, and much restored since.

Right: Before the construction of Wellington Road (North and South) as the town's first bypass route in 1826, the main north-south road through the town was by Manchester Road (Heaton Chapel), Lancashire Hill, Tiviot Dale, Hillgate and Buxton Road, a route turnpiked in 1725. This illustration shows some of the old houses formerly to be seen in Hillgate.

Below: In the rapidly developing towns of the early nineteenth century there was a shortage of Anglican churches to serve the growing population. In 1818 Parliament provided £1m for the building of new churches in these areas; they became known as Commissioners churches. Designed by George Basavi and built 1822-25, St Thomas's could accommodate almost 2,000 people. It was built facing Hillgate, then the main route through the town, but just after it opened, Wellington Road was itself opened, in 1826 and this took traffic away from Hillgate, and the church found itself facing the wrong way! This postcard view dates from around 1910.

This is the original Trinity Methodist church, built on Wellington Road South in stone in 1885 and opened on Thursday 21 January 1886. It seated 1124 people. The architects were Messrs William Waddington and Sons, of Manchester and Burnley.

Right: A view of the organ, presented by Mr Thomas Bayley, and opened on Sunday 11 September 1887 by Col. S.W. Wilkinson, a local musician.

Opposite: Described by the *Illustrated London News* as 'one of the finest churches in all England', St George's church on Buxton Road was consecrated by the Bishop of Chester on 25 February 1897; the architect was Herbert Austin. The first vicar was the Revd John Thorpe, the grandfather of the former leader of the Liberal Party, Mr Jeremy Thorpe. The Revd Arthur Symonds, the Vicar of St Thomas's, was regarded by some parishioners as too High Church, so they broke away and formed this new church and parish in Heaviley. The bulk of the cost was met by Major George Fearn. The church has ten bells and is larger than St. Mary's; the height of the spire is 230ft. This illustration is from an early postcard.

Above: That first church was demolished in 1971 after standing derelict for a long time. Its replacement was this building on Bramhall Lane South, Woodsmoor, built on Mount Tabor Memorial Playing Fields, and opened for worship in 1971. It was remodelled in its present form in 1986.

Opposite below: A postcard view of Bridge Street, *c.* 1910. The policeman on point duty seems somewhat lonely!

Right: Mealhouse Brow in June 1979 showing the Sun Inn building and the old dungeon, which was described as a 'little Roome under the said Oulde Courthouse' in a deed dated 1692. A century later, in 1790, the town's gaol was situated at the top of Mealhouse Brow, on the south side of the Market Place.

Below left: During the rebuilding of Mealhouse Brow part of Stockport's medieval town wall was exposed; this photograph dates from July 2005.

Below right: Rebuilding Castle Yard in May 2003.

Left and opposite: Staircase House, formerly known as Staircase Café, dates from around 1460. This medieval house originally had four timber A-frames, or crucks, and although the house was later altered, the two central crucks survived. It is the oldest known surviving town house of that period in Stockport. These two photographs are from 1970, before restoration.

The highly carved staircase, from which the building got its name, seen here in a nineteenth-century print, was inserted in the seventeenth century. It was unfortunately damaged by fire started by vandals in 1995.

The front of the building, seen here under repair in 1995. Stockport Heritage Trust successfully opposed the demolition of Staircase House, and following restoration by the local authority and with the assistance of National Lottery Funds, it re-opened in 2005. The rooms are furnished to show how it may have looked from its beginning until the 1940s. A permanent exhibition, 'The Stockport Story', opened in March 2006 in the adjoining building.

The original Tiviot Dale Chapel, seen here in 1970, erected 1825-26, was brick-built but with a stone façade. The road outside the chapel was originally the main road, and it remained as a through route until the 1980s, as the road direction signs indicate, when the M63 was extended as far as Portwood, severing the Tiviot Dale-Lancashire Hill road. The chapel was closed in 1971, to be replaced in 1972 by the present building.

Mersey Square was originally a public open space on each side of the Mersey adjacent to Wellington Bridge. Each side was linked by a new bridge in around 1900. This early postcard shows the Square at about this time; the Central Fire Brigade Station, on the left, with its distinctive tower, opened in 1902.

Town centre improvements of 1935 included covering over the river between the two bridges to create the present open space popularly known as the 'Bear Pit'. This photograph is from 1983, but the area is changing again under the latest (2006) redevelopment plans.

Left: The new and pedestrianised Merseyway Shopping Precinct (1961) took its name from the new road through the town created in 1935 when the section of the river between Mersey Square and Lancashire Bridge was built over. The original scheme included access between the two levels of the precinct by this escalator which has now been removed. The Co-op building (with the clock tower) is now called the Westgate Department Store.

Below: The Stockport War Memorial Art Gallery, built on the site of the old grammar school, was opened on 15 October 1925 by Prince Henry, Duke of Gloucester. It cost £24,000, raised entirely by voluntary donations, and is of Portland stone. Designed in the Greek style, it is a truly magnificent memorial to the 2,200 local men who gave their lives in the First World War and who are listed in the glass-roofed Hall of Memory. After the Second World War a further 780 names of local service men and women, and also civilians, who died during that conflict were added. This photograph, from 1970, was taken before the building was extended.

Above: Men from Stockport Corporation's Transport Department and the Town Hall section of the 38th Cheshire Battalion, Home Guard, are seen here in a photograph taken outside the Town Hall, *c.* 1940.

Below: It was not always work for the town's employees. As the caption to this image reveals, these are employees of Stockport Corporation's Transport Department (bus, tram and garage staff) on a visit to the Dunlop Rubber Co. Ltd.

Men of the Transport Department's football team who were the champions of the Inter-Departmental League in 1931. The man with the cup is Walter Smurthwaite, (captain), and on his left is Tommy Tumbelty, a conductor. Behind him is Sam Evison, clerk, and at the left of this row, Stanley Ellis, another clerk. On the far left of the photograph, behind the child, is Harry Russell, chief clerk at the Gas Department (competition organiser). Next to him, with a scarf, is Jimmy Heywood, who played full-back for Stockport County, and the man with the cap in the centre is Harold Wheeler, a conductor and the team's trainer. Sammy Monks is third from the right.

The Transport Department's football team posed for this evocative photograph outside the Waggon and Horses in Hazel Grove in 1909.

Each year a Civic Service is held at St Mary's parish church to celebrate the election of the incoming mayor. Here, in 1970, the Civic Party is led by the Mayor, Alderman James G. Walton, and the Town Clerk, Mr D.W. Hay, with the Market Hall as a backdrop.

Stockport Historical Interest Society was founded in 1961 and here, the renamed Stockport Historical Society, launches its publication *Morning's Walk*, June 1974. In the frame are, left to right, Shirley McKenna (hon. secretary), Cllr Harry Walker, Jim Hooley (d. 21 June 2003, aged 89) and Jeffrey Morgan-Lewis (chairman).

Members of the Stockport Historical Society celebrating its eighteenth birthday in February 1979.

Stockport Cricket Club, Second Eleven team, champions of Division Two of the Central Lancashire League in 1941. They defeated Heywood Second Eleven by four wickets at Heywood on Saturday 13 September. Heywood scored 132 (E. Williams 5-26) in reply to Stockport's 140-6 (T.C. Keen, 59 not out). The team, photographed at Heywood, are: back row, left to right: G. Riddell, E. Williams, T.W. Jones, P. Edge, J. Hooley, R. Webb. Front row: F. Dranfield, R.W. Hall, F.W. Archer, E.F. Burn (captain), R.A. Martin and T.C. Keen.

Stockport Cricket Club, Second Eleven again, this time as winners of the Whittaker Cup and joint champions of Division Two of the Central Lancashire League in 1944. They won the Whittaker Cup by defeating Heywood Second Eleven (again!) by five wickets. Stockport made 120-5 (innings closed, Peter Urmston 63) but Heywood could only make 74 (Gorton Peters, captain of Rossall School, taking 5-24, and T.W. Jones 3-19). The *Heywood Advertiser*'s match report (22 September 1944) says that the home team 'proved no match for Stockport…at Crimble last Saturday'. Stockport had previously defeated Heywood twice in league matches. The Cup was presented to the Stockport captain, W.R. Hall, by Mr H. Johnson of Royton. The team tied for the League Championship with Oldham and it was agreed that each club would hold the championship trophy for six months.

The First Eleven beat Milnrow at Cale Green by two wickets on 3 September 1949 to finish level on points with them. They drew the play-off at Milnrow a week later and the clubs were declared joint champions of the First Division of the Central Lancashire League. The captain, Alan Chapman, won the toss to decide who held the Championship first and was presented with the Championship Cup and flag. As with the Second Eleven in 1941, in 1949 Stockport had defeated Milnrow twice in league matches.

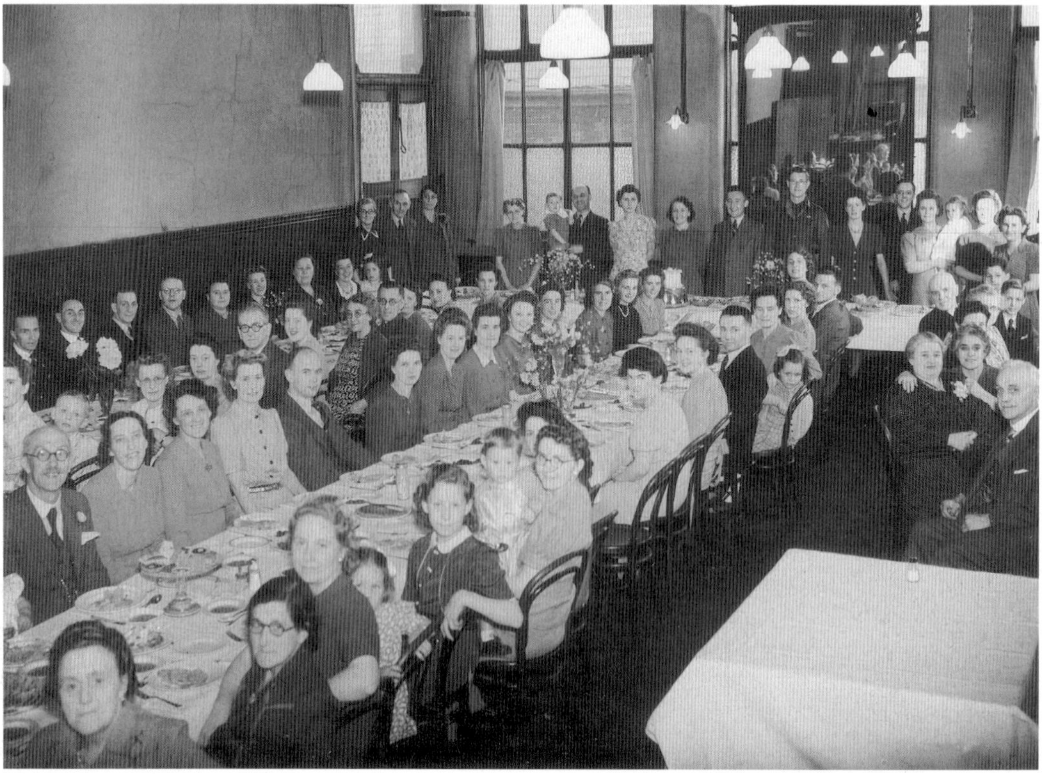

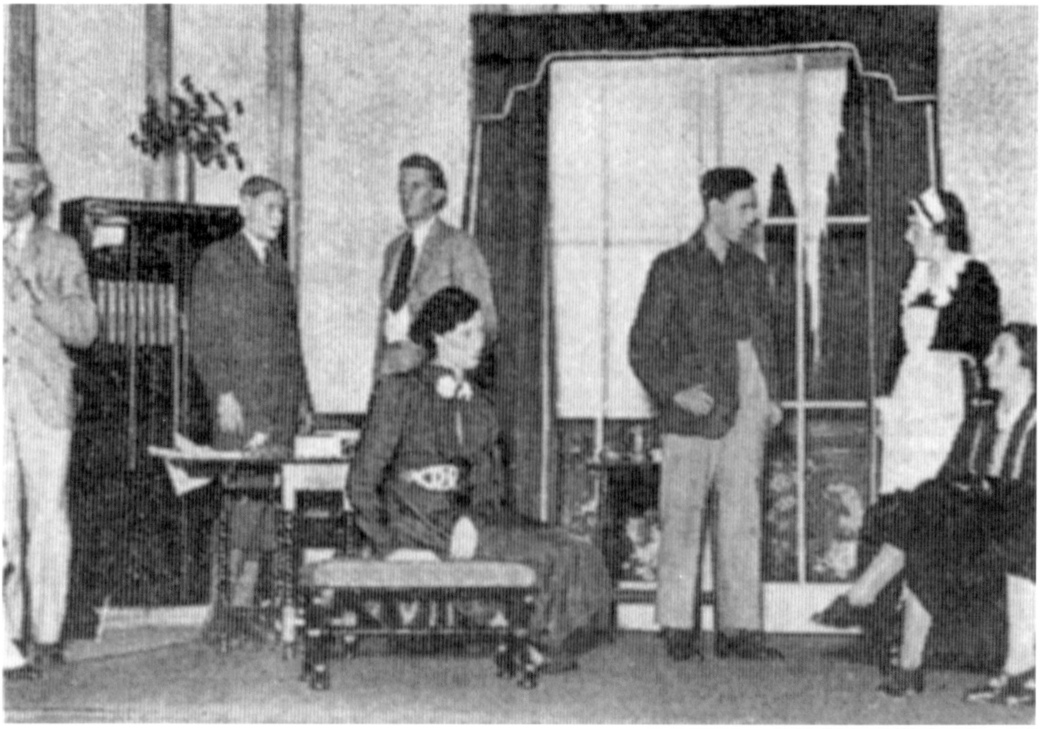

Offerton Hall came into the ownership of the Wright family on the marriage of Ann Bradshaw and Laurence Wright. The house was rebuilt or remodelled early in the eighteenth century. A later Wright, William, was Lord of Offerton and Mottram St Andrew and a wealthy landowner. He paid for St Peter's church in Stockport in 1768 and the road now known as St Petersgate. This view dates from April 1977.

Opposite above: A 'Victory in Europe' Day celebratory tea in Crossley's Café, Vernon Park, on 11 June 1945.

Opposite below: The Roundabout by J.B. Priestley was presented by the Stockport Seconians Association (Stockport Secondary School) drama group in the Garrick Hall in November 1936, produced by Mr Ernest F. Burn. The players in this scene are, left to right: Herbert Thorpe (Lord Kettlewell), Robert Hardie (Churton Saunders), Fred Swinfin (Alec Grenside), Aileen Twiss (Pamela Kettlewell), Stanley Bowden (Comrade Staggles), Mary Ridyard (Alice), and Mary Martin (Hilda Lancicourt).

Above and below: In the 1980s a number of alternative schemes for road improvements were under consideration both by the government and local residents, who favoured what was called 'the blue route'. Offerton Community Council revived the May Day Festival in 1987, both as a community entertainment and as a means of engaging local support. Here, on May Day 1988 are recorded some of the scenes at that year's event. Today, almost twenty years later, a decision is still awaited!

This page and overleaf: Offerton residents and participants enjoying themselves on May Day 1989.

Opposite below: Great Moor was by far the largest expanse of common land in the township of Stockport, at over 100 acres in extent. Phyllis Giles's researches reveal that, apart from a little horse-racing, particularly in the 1760s, it was 'a wild and desolate spot ... avoided at night'. A gibbet stood on the edge of the Black Lake (the area between Cherry Tree Lane and Dialstone Lane) where criminals were hung up in chains as recently as the 1790s. During the meetings of the Enclosure Committee in 1805, Dial Stone Road became the principal public highway (twenty yards wide) and Cherry Tree Lane and Lisburn Lane were among other public roads created at the time. As late as the 1850s the area was still largely rural, drainage problems hindering its development; in this postcard view from around 1910, local residents are drawn to the presence of the photographer!

Above: This photograph is from around 1930 and is thought to be Offerton Cricket Club, as my contributor identifies 'Stan and Dad' on the front row. Stan Riddell is the fourth from the left, with his half-brother, Arthur Riddell, fifth from the left.

The population of Reddish dramatically increased in the nineteenth century and consequently so did the need for a cemetery. The Willow Grove Cemetery Company was formed to purchase the Willow Grove House and estate from local manufacturer Joseph Marsland. The site originally included a chapel and a mortuary building. The first interment was on 19 November 1877. The cemetery was purchased by the local authority in 1972 for £3,500 and a programme of restoration was begun. This view of the cemetery is from an early coloured postcard.

two

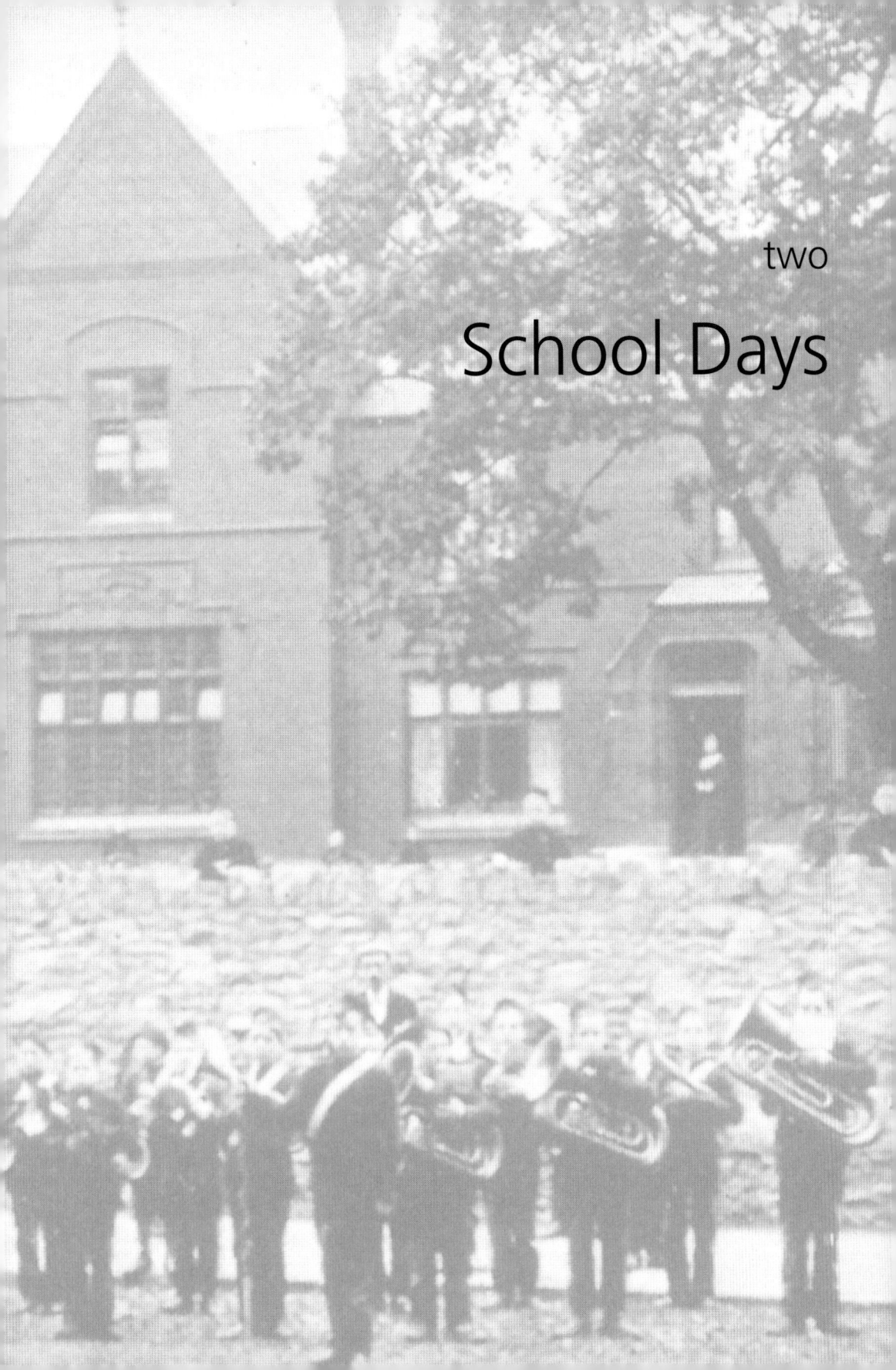

School Days

Throughout the Victorian period, education for everyone, as a national aim, slowly developed; it was not compulsory until late in her reign. In 1833 the government granted £20,000 for the 'erection of school houses', a grant increased in 1839 to £30,000. Under Graham's Factory Act of 1844, factory children under thirteen years of age were to be 'half-timers', i.e. they spent half a day in the factory and the other half at school. Two years later the Whigs introduced their pupil-teacher scheme at an initial cost of £100,000. Under this scheme the brightest children assisted the regular teacher. In 1856 the Department of Education was established, and reports on Elementary Education (1861), Public Schools (1864) and Secondary Schools (1868), paved the way for the Education Act of 1870.

William Edward Forster, MP for Bradford, had been made Vice-President of the Department of Education by the Prime Minister, William Ewart Gladstone. Forster had been an active educationalist for many years. He had started a school for half-timers in a woollen mill he partly owned, and he favoured financing schools by both rates and taxes. Non-sectarian and undenominational schools, run by School Boards, were introduced. Parents deemed too poor were excused from paying the fees known as 'school pence'. School attendance for all children from five to twelve years of age became compulsory. Church schools continued to receive state funding. The Act became law on 9 August 1870.

The Anniversary Celebrations

Programme of Events

June 19th Friday	Official opening of the Anniversary Exhibition. At 3-00 p.m. in the War Memorial Art Gallery. The Exhibition will remain open until July 11th.
	750th Anniversary Banquet. At the Town Hall at 7-30 p.m.
June 20th Saturday	Beating the Retreat, by the Mercian Volunteers. In the Merseyway Precinct at 6-30 p.m.
June 21st Sunday	Civic Service at St. Mary's Parish Church at 11-00 a.m. With a procession from the Town Hall at 10-30 a.m.
June 22nd Monday	Schools Dance Festival. At the Town Hall at 7-30 p.m. This event is also part of the celebrations of the Centenary of the 1870 Education Act.
June 23rd Tuesday	Concert by the B.B.C. Northern Orchestra. At the Town Hall at 7-30 p.m.
June 24th Wednesday	Seven centuries of the Stockport sound. An entertainment by the Stockport Federation of Cultural Societies. At the Town Hall at 7-30 p.m.
June 25th Thursday	Concert by the Stockport Youth Orchestra. At the Town Hall at 7-30 p.m. This concert is also part of the celebrations of the Centenary of the 1870 Education Act.
June 26th Friday	Anniversary Concert by the Fairey Band. At the Town Hall at 7-30 p.m.

Many Corporation departments will be open to the public from June 22nd — 26th, and there will be special activities at the schools.

Left: 1970 was the centenary of the Education Act which, among other provisions, made attendance at school compulsory for all for the first time and in Stockport, as elsewhere, there was a programme of events to celebrate the Act. This programme lists the events held in Stockport in celebration of the centenary.

Opposite above: Stockport Sunday School was established in 1806 in Lower Hillgate, and on 5 October 1907 the foundation stone of Centenary Hall was laid by Mrs Henry Bell, the mayoress. The building opened on 9 October 1909. This photograph of the Hall is from 1970.

Opposite below: Children progressed from the beginner's class, through the infants, junior and intermediate departments, until going up to the teenager's class in 'The Large Room'. Centenary Hall was noted for its 'wonderful and perfect acoustics' for worship, music (the Halle Orchestra appeared here), drama and public meetings and lectures of all kinds. This photograph, from February 1971, shows demolition work in progress.

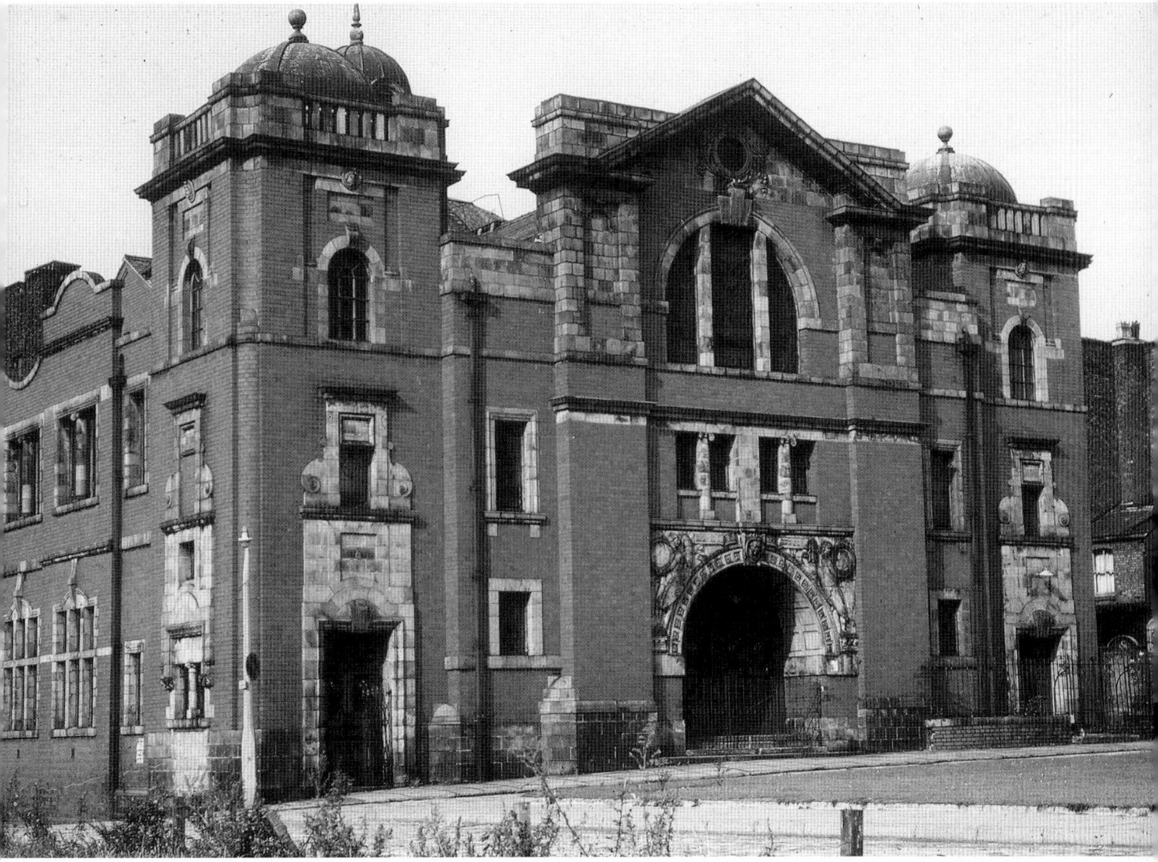

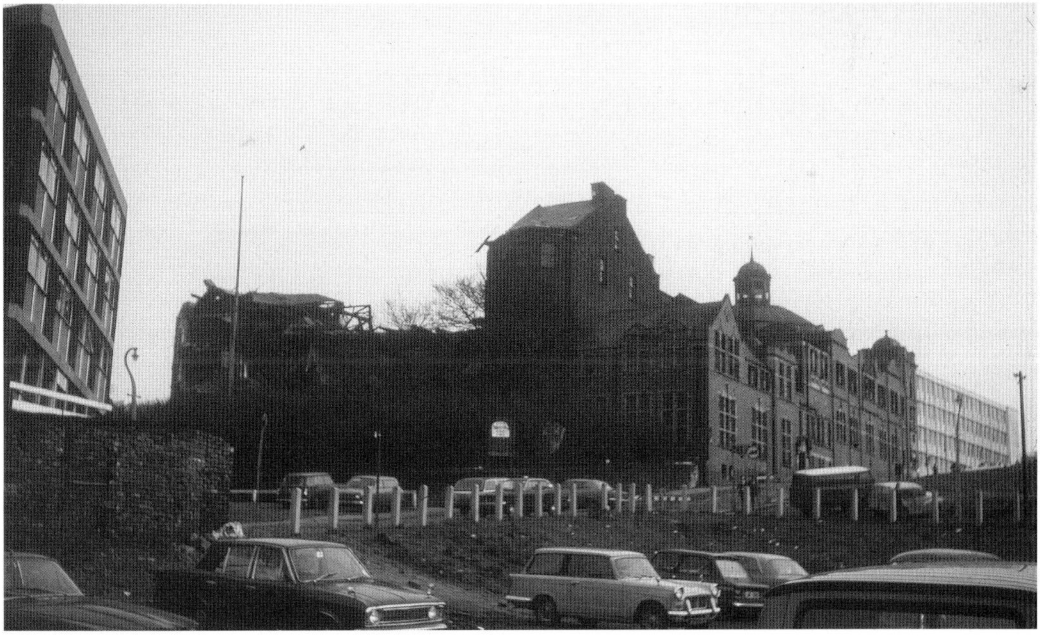

Above and below: Stockport Technical School opened on Greek Street in 1889, providing joinery and engineering workshops, art and metallurgical rooms and a dyehouse; a weaving shed was added later. Reorganised as Stockport College of Further Education in 1927, it had 1,700 students by 1935. By the 1990s, now developed as Stockport College of Further and Higher Education, it had 15,000 students. This year (2006) plans have been announced for its further growth and development. These photographs date from 1970.

Above and below: These two class photographs from Banks Lane Council School are from 1932–33. Unfortunately, I have no names for either the teachers or the pupils.

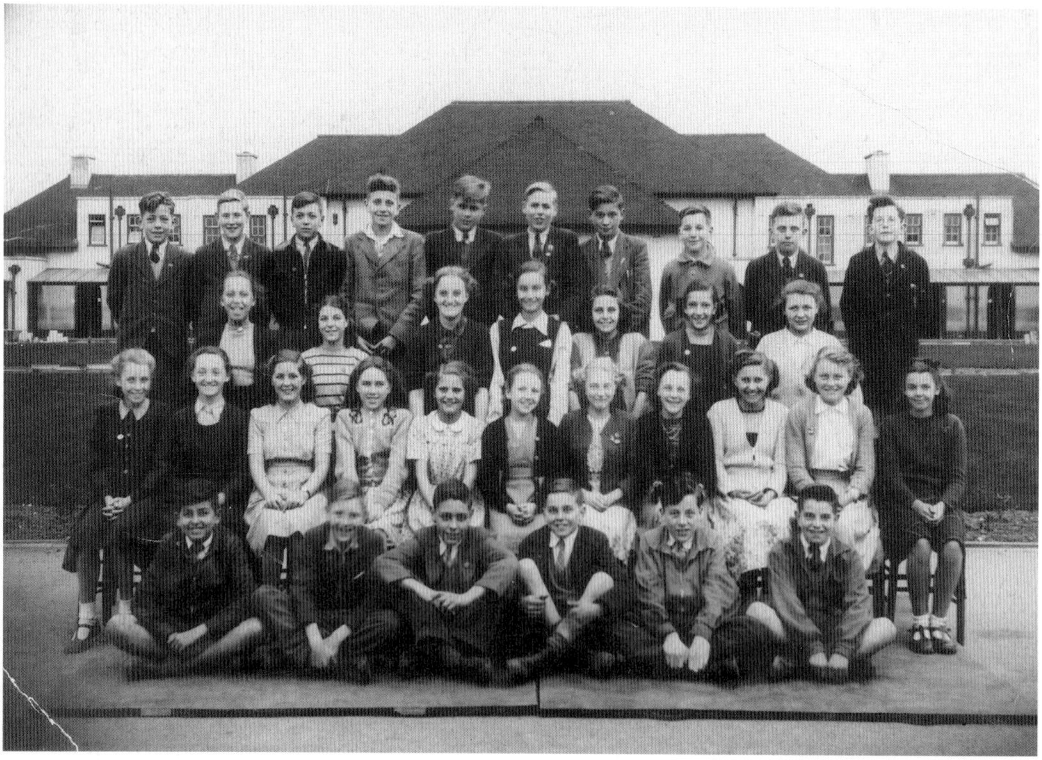

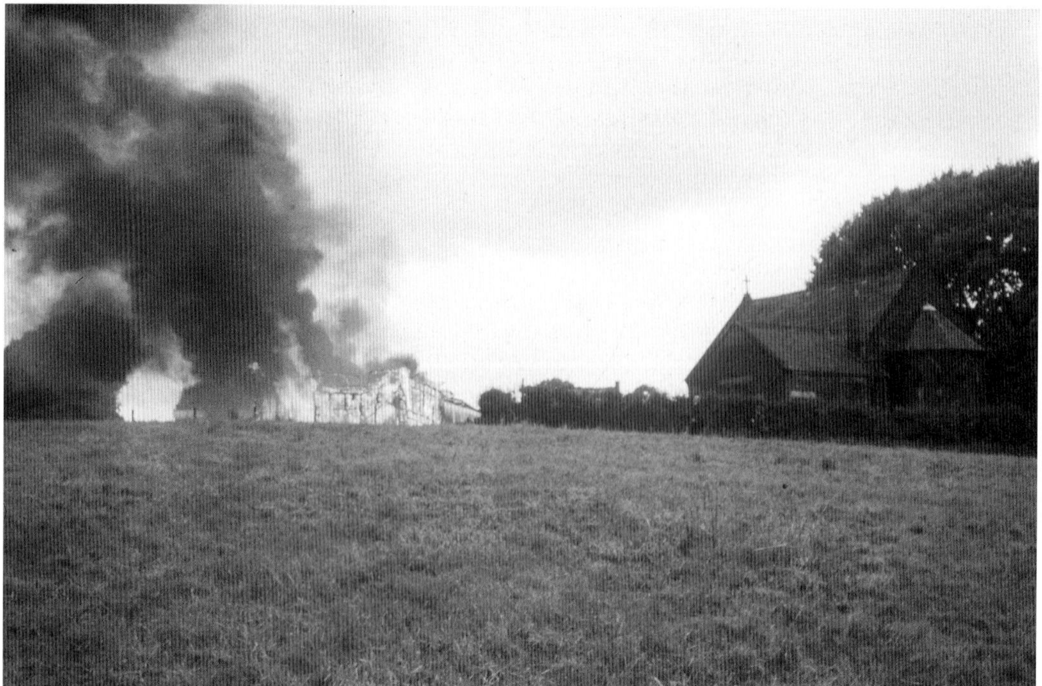

Above: In 1897 two industrial schools opened in Offerton, one for 150 boys, on Marple Road, the other, on Dialstone Lane, for 60 girls. Both schools were managed by a committee under the Certified Industrial Schools Act. The boys' school, seen here, was built as a home and school to educate orphans and delinquent boys. It fulfilled this function until it was taken over by the local health authority in 1950, when it became a home, known as Offerton House, for people with learning difficulties. Following its demolition, the site is now used for housing and some community facilities. The home for girls later became a social club for staff of Battersby's. The building survives today as the Britannia Hotel.

Opposite above: Class 3B of Dialstone Secondary Modern School, in Lisburn Lane, Offerton, in October 1950. This school opened in April 1934 as Dialstone Central School. The scheme was to build a number of these Central Schools, but only Dialstone was completed. By 1954 it had 840 pupils. In that year it was divided: the boys remained here, in Dialstone Secondary Modern School for Boys, while the girls went to the newly-completed Offerton Secondary Modern Girls' School. Back row, left to right: James Slater, Keith Fletcher, Derek Pollit, -?-, -?-, -?-, -?-, Jim Gilman, David Walker, David Caton. Third row: Sheila Brown, Dorothy Aspland, Ann Stanley, Cynthia Dickinson, -?-, -?-, Margaret Wood. Second row: Pat Seward, Pat Stewart, Dorothy Chatfield, Maureen Casey, Hilda Pedley, Mavis Hall, Audrey ?, Pauline Wilkinson, Jean Smith, Sylvia Butler, Gillian Bradbrooke; Front row: Olwyn Lee, Cliff Nicholls, Keith Baird, Russell Bamber, -?-, John Astle.

Opposite below: Photographed in May 1971, one of a number of pre-fabricated buildings erected to cope with increasing demand at St John's church school, Offerton (right) is on fire. The foundation stone had been laid in 1876 by Mrs Bradshaw-Isherwood, of Marple Hall and it closed in the 1980s.

Above: Following the success of the Stockport Sunday School, several branch or auxiliary schools were established. In Heaton Mersey a new purpose-built school was erected by Robert Parker in 1805.

Opposite below, left and right: These two photographs show the entrance to the school and, in greater detail, the notice board.

Right: Inside the school was a memorial tablet to its founder, Robert Parker, who took over the bleach works, established locally in the 1780s by the brothers Samuel and Thomas Oldknow. Later, he added spinning and weaving operations at the works.

Below: Standard 4 or 5 of St John's School, Heaton Mersey in around 1909. St John's church was completed in 1850, the school was built in 1857 and an infant school was added in 1869.

IN
MEMORY OF
ROBERT PARKER, ESQ[r]
Who died July 21st A.D.1813
Æt. 70 years.
He founded this
SUNDAY SCHOOL,
for the Education
and Religious Instruction
of the rising generation
A.D.1806.
And afterwards
Bequeathed to it the Sum of
Five Hundred Pounds
for its perpetual Support.

This Token
of grateful respect
was erected by
the TEACHERS and SCHOLARS
A.D.1823.

What became Oriel Bank High School was founded in 1887 by Miss Shaw in a house at the corner of Kennerley Road, Davenport. When new shop developments began here the school moved across the road to the house next to 'Bramhall Mount'. Following further expansion it moved to No. 12 Devonshire Park Road, the former home of Dr and Mrs Main, and later acquired the adjoining property, No. 10, which had been a dwelling house, then a private hotel, and then the nurses' home for Stepping Hill Hospital. Over the years additional facilities were provided. It had been co-educational in the past but more recently it became a girls only school. It closed in 2005. At the 1990 Independent Schools Association Drama Festival, held on Saturday 17 March at Crewe, the School's entry won the cup for the second year in succession, and Victoria Browne, as Herald, won 'best actress in a supporting role'. The play was called *All the King's Men* and the cast was: Rachel Blackie (Dr Chillingworth), Nesta Hoare (King Charles I), Amanda Walker (Queen Henrietta), Katie Fairbottom (Colonel Massey), Christine Bottomley (Drummer Boy), Victoria Browne (Herald), Emma Walker (Messenger). It was produced by Mrs Watkins and the musicians were Mrs Beaumont, Victoria Browne, Christine Bottomley and Emma Knott.

Oriel Bank High School
Headmistress Mrs. A. P. Perrett, B.A.

Right: From the cover of one of those dreaded school form reports!

three

Hatting, Brewing and Other Industries

'Here are foundries, machine works, breweries and flour mills, but the staple trade of the town is the spinning and manufacture of cotton and the making of hats.' This picture of Stockport's industrial base comes from Kelly's *Directory of Cheshire* (1910 ed.)

Although hatting in Stockport can be traced back to the sixteenth century, its heyday was the nineteenth and early twentieth centuries. In 1851 there were only nineteen hatters, but this number increased to thirty-one 'hat manufacturers' and twelve 'hatters' by 1887. Some of these were large concerns such as Christys and Carringtons; other well-known firms were Battersby & Co. (founded 1865), T. & W. Lees (1870) and Minshulls (*c.* 1872). By the end of the nineteenth century some 10,000 people were employed in this industry alone.

In brewing, one of the first commercial enterprises was the Portwood Brewery, established in about 1796, to be followed in the nineteenth century by such well-know names as Bell's and the Brookfield brewery (both on Hempshaw Lane), Clarke's (South Reddish), Robinson's Unicorn Brewery and the Windsor Castle Brewery in Edgeley, and the Royal Oak Brewery on Higher Hillgate.

Above: Battersby and Co. began in 1865 and moved to purpose-built premises on Hempshaw Lane, Offerton, in 1886. By the 1890s they had over 1,000 employees. The tall water tower was added when the premises were rebuilt in 1906 following a disastrous fire. When the firm, by then part of Associated British Hat Manufacturers Ltd, closed, the premises became a temporary Hat Museum. This photograph shows Battersby's hatworks in October 1980.

Opposite below: Battersby's playing away! Here, in 1936, Battersby's treat their workers to a dinner in the Winter Gardens at Blackpool.

Right: This is part of the temporary display at the museum in February 1997. On show is machinery from Plant's hatworks. This firm was founded by William Plant (1804-1881) in 1828 in Churchgate Mill as hat block and woodcraft manufacturers. The business was continued by his two sons Henry (1837-1921) and William (1845-1915). He also had eleven other children! William and his son William James (1877-1970) set up their own factory in Hilton Street, Manchester and from 1902-1976 they were at 67A Great Ancoats Street, Manchester. William James's brother, Walter Plant, born in 1885, died in 1976, aged 91, and his daughter, Miss Aileen Plant, donated the entire contents of his office and workshops to Stockport Museum. Stockport's Hat Museum opened in Wellington Mill in 2000, the former hat works of Ward Brothers.

Battersby's concert party group was known as 'The Bigshots'.

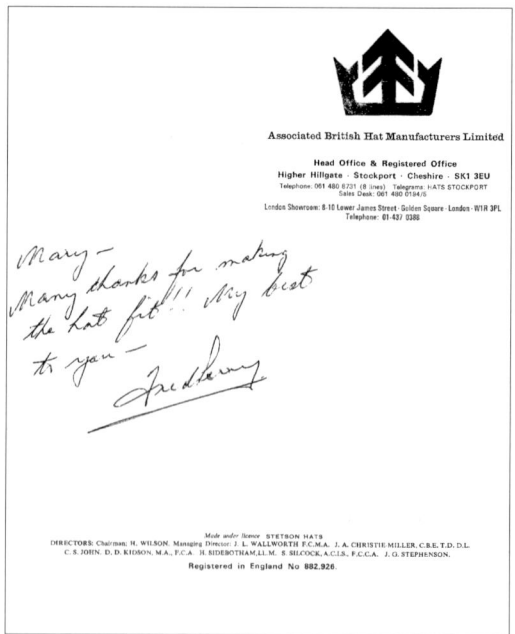

Above left: Their London warehouse was established in 1897 and this advertisement, from the same year, shows the Hempshaw Lane works, Offerton.

Above right: An example of Associated British Hat Manufacturers Ltd headed notepaper with a complimentary note (and autograph) from Fred Perry, the local tennis player and last British winner of the Mens' Singles Final at Wimbledon in 1937.

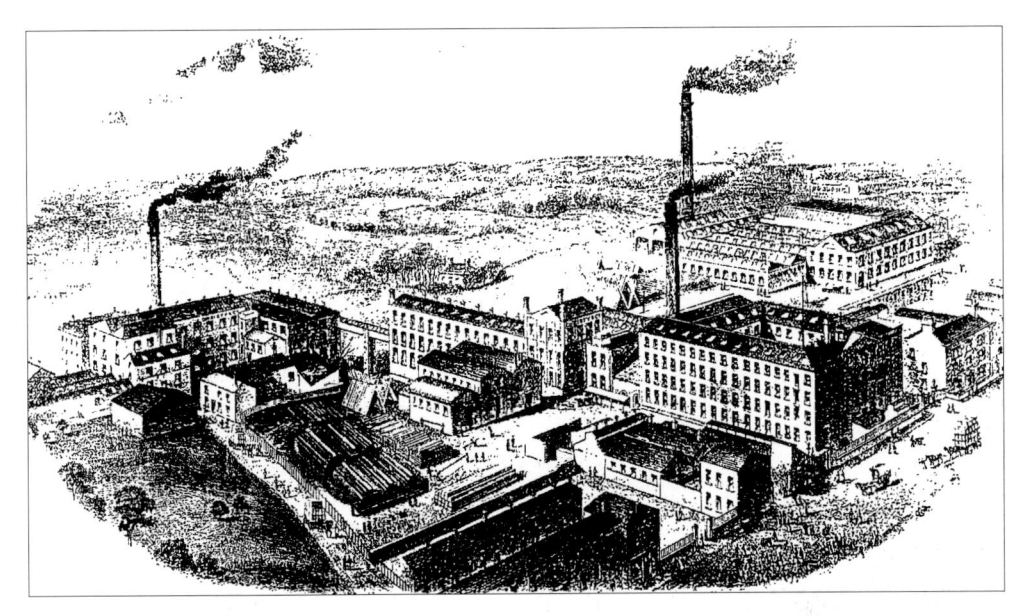

This line drawing gives a representation of how Christy's hat works looked in about 1890. The original Hillgate Mill is to the right with, behind it, the recently-erected South Mill (1873); Canal Street works are to the left. The site is thought to have been the most extensive hat factory in Europe. There were sheds for blacksmiths, block turners and dye stores, it covered an area of 11 acres and employed over 1,500 workers. As part of Associated British Hat Manufacturers, Christy's finally closed in December 1997, so marking the end of the hat industry in the town.

This illustration, from about 1880, shows Minshall's premises at Carrington Field. The firm lasted until the early twentieth century and remained a family-run business.

Left: In the nineteenth century Stockport had six major breweries: Bell's, the Brookfield, Clarke's, Robinson's, Windsor Castle and the Royal Oak. Now only Robinson's is still operating. The firm began in the old Unicorn Inn on Hillgate in the 1830s. This inn is first recorded in 1724 and it ceased after the close of business on 31 December 1935; the site is now the brewery's yard. The first Robinson brewer had previously been a cotton spinner. The family slowly built up a chain of pubs, eventually acquiring Kay's 'Atlas' Brewery, of Hyde, and with it, Bakers Vaults. More importantly, perhaps, they acquired Bells (Hempshaw Lane) who had many pubs especially in Hazel Grove. Robinson's is still very much a private company and a family firm. The Unicorn Brewery is seen in this photograph in June 1977.

Below left and right: Before the advent of motorised transport, goods were moved and delivered in a variety of horse-drawn vehicles. In the brewing trade the carts were called drays and even today they can be seen on our roads. The first picture is from May 1980 and the second, in Dial Park Road, September 1980. Long may Robinsons and their drays be with us!

Above and below: A sequence of Stockport pubs! The Turners, like the Bakers, were mainly wine and spirit merchants; their distillery was the building with the covered steps alongside. They acquired the Queen's Head in 1809. The present Turner's Vaults is in reality a fragment of the old Queen's Head. This pub was first recorded in 1794 though it is thought to have received its licence when the ancient Royal Oak, which dated from at least 1680, was demolished. Both photographs are from March 1978.

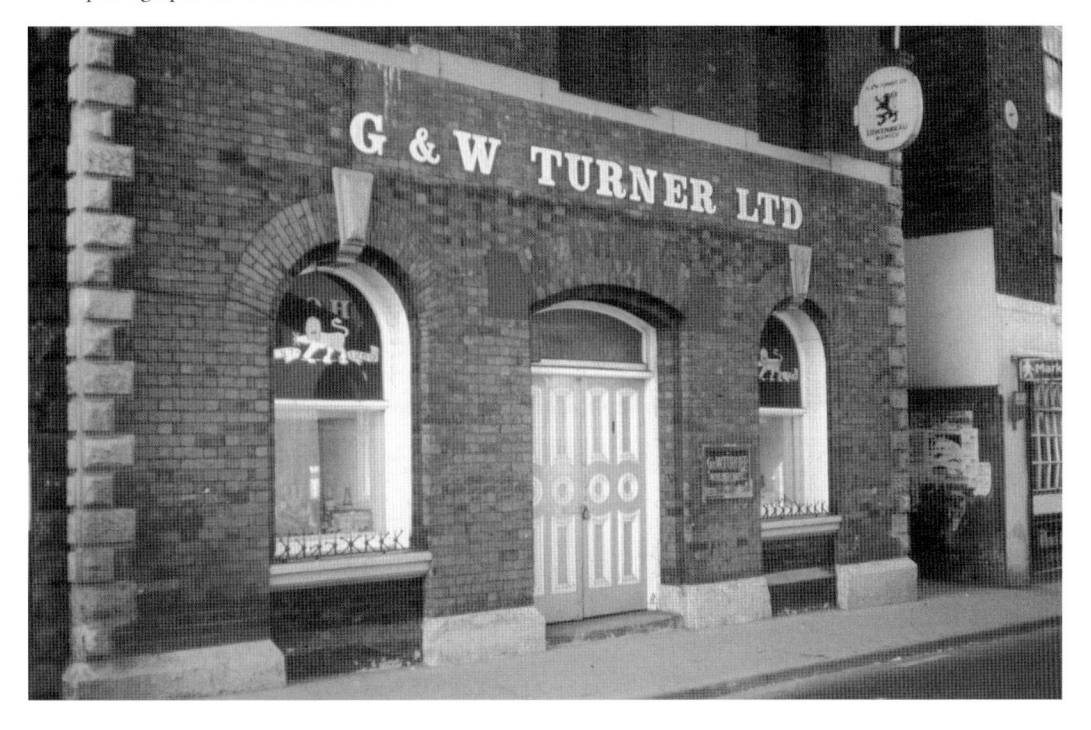

Left: Baker's Vaults, Market Place. Formerly called the George and Dragon, this was first mentioned in 1820, it was rebuilt in around 1860 and re-named The Baker's Vaults at that time. It originally extended into Market Place but when the covered market was built its frontage was set back. The Baker family, mainly wine merchants, owned much of the Market (Bridge Street) Brow and owned the inn from about 1824 for about fifty years.

Below: The Millstone Inn, 112 Lancashire Hill. Up to the nineteenth century a windmill stood on Lancashire Hill. It is thought that the inn's name comes from the fact that Nelstrop's Albion Flour Mill is almost opposite where the Millstone Inn used to be. The inn was closed and demolished in 1967 and its existence is commemorated in the new flats called Stonemill Terrace.

Above: The Rope and Anchor, 12 Park Street, was first recorded in 1824. It may have been the meeting place of the Court Leet. It closed in 1939 and is seen here in 1940. It was later converted into a café-restaurant which, reflecting the clientele, was nick-named the 'Lads' Club'.

Right: The Tim Bobbin Inn is first mentioned in 1820 and is pictured here a century later in 1920. The name commemorates the Lancashire dialect poet John Collier alias Tim Bobbin (1708-1786) who published a volume of verse in 1768. The pub closed in December 1927. The pawnbroker's sign is for E. Ormisher, No. 5 London Place.

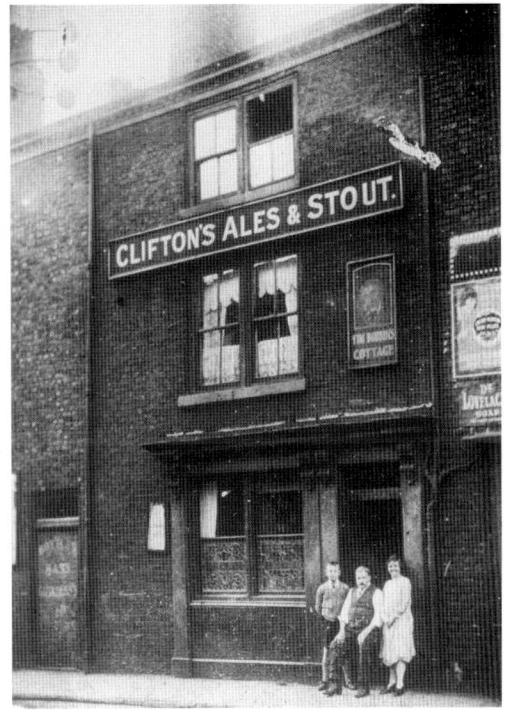

The Vernons inherited the Barony and Manor of Stockport from the Warrens in 1826 and the Vernon Arms is first mentioned in the following year. It closed in 1975, its licence being transferred to the Puss in Boots on Nangreave Road, built that year. The Vernon Arms had some marvellous glazed screens and a fine painted sign, and 'good stabling'.

First mentioned in 1838, when the licensee was Abraham Unsworth, the Mersey Inn was rebuilt in gin-palace style. It assumed the name Mersey Hotel in 1895 and became the Mersey Tavern in 1972. In this photograph from 1895 we see Chestergate at its former level and the elevated roadway is the present level.

This photograph is from 1970. More recently, The Mersey Tavern has changed its name again, to The Chestergate.

The Crown Inn, Heaton Mersey, is first mentioned in records in 1791. The licence may have lapsed, for the proprietor of the nearby bleach works strongly objected to a proposal in September 1833 to convert it into a 'Tom and Gerry' house. Under the 1831 Truck Act, wages had to be paid wholly in cash rather than partly in vouchers, which could only be redeemed at a company outlet. Beautifully preserved, it is now part of a conservation area on Didsbury Road and is seen here in April 1978.

This very old-established coaching inn, the Crown Inn, Great Moor, was rebuilt in 1928, though its origins may go back to *c.* 1666-7. It had a famous and very popular bowling green.

As the William IV, this pub was first recorded in 1838 (he reigned 1830-37), but took its present name, the Church Inn, in 1851 when St Paul's church, designed by Messrs Bowman and Crowther, was built nearby. The last service at St Paul's was on 8 August 1971 and it was demolished in 1974. This photograph of the Church Inn, which was in Great Portwood Street, dates from April 1979.

I don't know who this young man is, but in Kelly's *Directory of Cheshire* (1910 ed.), Johnson Brothers (Dyers) Ltd, dyers and cleaners, are listed as being at 5 Little Underbank – could this be where the photograph was taken?

By 1794 John Collier had built two water-powered mills opposite each other, with a weir between them across the River Mersey. Dr Arrowsmith records that 'the lower part of one of these two wheelhouses, at the aptly named Weir (or Wear) Mill, still survives, and is possibly Stockport's oldest remaining mill structure'. This photograph of Weir (or Wear) Mill is from April 1977.

This 'fireproof' mill dates from 1828 and was built by the wealthy industrialist Thomas Marsland. Brick vaulting, cast-iron beams, and roof-trusses also of cast-iron (an unusual feature) made Wellington Mill a very safe structure. It is one of Stockport's tallest industrial buildings, its seven storeys rising majestically over Daw Bank bus station. It was used for weaving and spinning and was later used by Ward's, the hatting manufacturer. Today it is the home of Stockport's award-winning Hat Museum and is pictured here in April 1977.

Orrell's Mill, a six-storied, 'fireproof' cotton mill, was built by William Fairburn, the well-known Manchester engineer, 1834-1835, in Travis Street, Heaton Mersey. It contained spinning machinery, with 35,000 spindles and 1,100 power looms. Dr Andrew Ure, in his book *The Cotton manufacture in Great Britain*, published in 1836, shows looms on the ground floor, throstle frames on the first and second floors, carding engines on the third floor and mules on the fourth and fifth floors. The main spinning rooms were 280 ft by 50 ft, with two rows of cast-iron columns. This view is from Brinksway Bridge and dates from April 1977. After severe damage by fire it was demolished early in 1980.

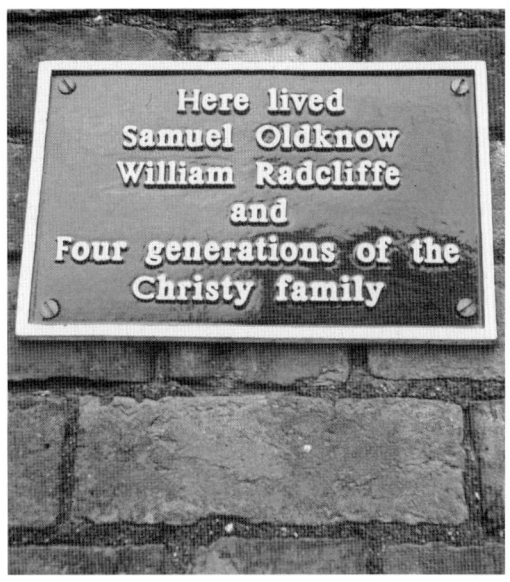

Above left: Oldknow's house, Higher Hillgate, photographed in 1977 at the time of the closure of Christy's hatting business. The house is currently (2006) in a very poor condition, the state of its interior being worse than was first thought, involving English Heritage in additional expense as restoration proceeds.

Above right: This plaque recorded the various occupants of the house, when it was used during Christy's time here as their office; a photograph from May 1980.

These old cottages in Vale Road, Heaton Mersey, are typical of those built by the Oldknows to house their workers in the 1820s and later. The bleach works, established in the 1780s, expanded greatly in the nineteenth century.

Above: These bleach workers' cottages may be in Park Row.

Left: The lower bleach works were later known as Melland and Coward's from the middle of the nineteenth century, and although there were later changes of ownership, their name remains associated with the works, which finally closed in 1992. The chimney, seen here in a photograph from April 1977, was at that time Stockport's tallest surviving mill chimney, but this was demolished in 1995.

four

Moving Around

By the end of the nineteenth century and the early years of the twentieth, the developing process of photography and the increasing number of postcard manufacturers were beginning to record images of practically every city, town and village in the country. The emphasis may have been on larger towns and villages, but even in the smallest communities there were people who were able to afford one of the new-fangled cameras and representatives of postcard manufacturers seem to have visited each and every community. Thankfully, for us a century later, we can still enjoy a wide range of these views – no limit, it seems, was placed on the variety of scenes recorded.

At the same time ordinary people were able to move about in a way that their parents would have found difficult and they got into the habit of either buying postcards for themselves as a record of places they visited, or of sending them to friends and relatives when they were away. While the majority of such cards may have been thrown away, enough survive today for us to see for ourselves what our locality looked like a century ago and how our forbears were able to get to work and go visiting.

Below: This image from a coloured postcard of around 1910 shows a tram on Wellington Road in Heaton Chapel.

Opposite above: : The location is Heaton Mersey and this is a horse-drawn coach on the service between Palatine Road and Cheadle. The driver is believed to be Mr Telford.

Opposite below: This horse-drawn tram was photographed near St Peter's church, Stockport.

Left: This is bus No. 116, registration No. DB 7462, and electric tram No. 53 photographed, probably, at the Mersey Square depot. Could the official-looking gentleman posing proudly here with the vehicles be the depot manager?

Below: This splendid photograph of tram No. 32 shows driver Arthur Jinks at the controls with guard David Knowles.

Opposite above: An early postcard view of Mersey Square, with electric trams. The first electric tram service in the town began in August 1901, when Stockport Corporation began a service to Reddish and Woodley. The first service between Stockport and Manchester dates from June in the following year, run by Manchester Corporation under an agreement with Stockport.

Opposite below: Electric trams did not start to run in Stockport until 26 August 1901. The first section of the Cheadle route was commissioned in January 1902 and was eventually linked with the Reddish service on 6 July 1903, to provide a cross-town service through Mersey Square. The date of the picture is probably from around that time. Why does the tram still carry a crown with the VR symbol when Queen Victoria had died on 22 January 1901?

VAUX'S STOUT
VAN HOUTEN'S COCOA

V R
CHEADLE STOCKPORT REDDISH
STOCKPORT CORPORATION TRAMW

Above: This photograph is thought to show the Corporation's first tramway office – the small lean-to structure - on Lancashire Bridge, and which apparently later became a barber's shop. The photograph must date from the period 1901 to 1909, that is, some time between the introduction of trams in 1901 and the erection of the Tramways Department's new offices in Mersey Square in 1909. Although an extensive search of maps, directories and other sources has been carried out, the exact location of this first office cannot be verified. It might possibly be at the north-west corner of Lancashire Bridge.

Above: An electric tram in Buxton Road – if only traffic levels now were as light as they were then!

Right: Dan Bank is part of the Stockport to Marple turnpike road. In 1792 Samuel Oldknow repaired and gravelled the road between Offerton and Marple at his own expense. The early motor buses would have found Dan Bank hard going, as indeed it can still be to some vehicles today.

Opposite below: This aerial photograph, taken in the 1960s (see the gantries on the viaduct for the newly-electrified railway) shows the Transport Department's offices and depot built in 1932. The tramway depot, right, was opened in January 1924, offices were provided in 1927 and the bus garage, with the clock tower, dates from July 1932. The Heaton Lane multi-storey car park now occupies this whole site.

The first horse-drawn omnibus service started as early as 1830 with a service between Stockport and Manchester. By the 1870s rival services were operating between Stockport and Hazel Grove – the current controversy regarding the 192 route is nothing new!

Electric tram No.35 at the Hazel Grove terminus with driver Barnett and guard Broadbent.

The Hazel Grove Tram and Carriage Company began their service into Stockport in 1890. Their premises, seen here, were behind the Crown Inn on London Road, Hazel Grove.

The location is Kennerley Road, Davenport, formerly called Kennerley Grove Lane, with two of the company's horse-drawn cars. Following the purchase of the company by Stockport Corporation the lines were electrified and opened for traffic on 5 July 1905.

STOCKPORT BULLOCK-SMITHIANS

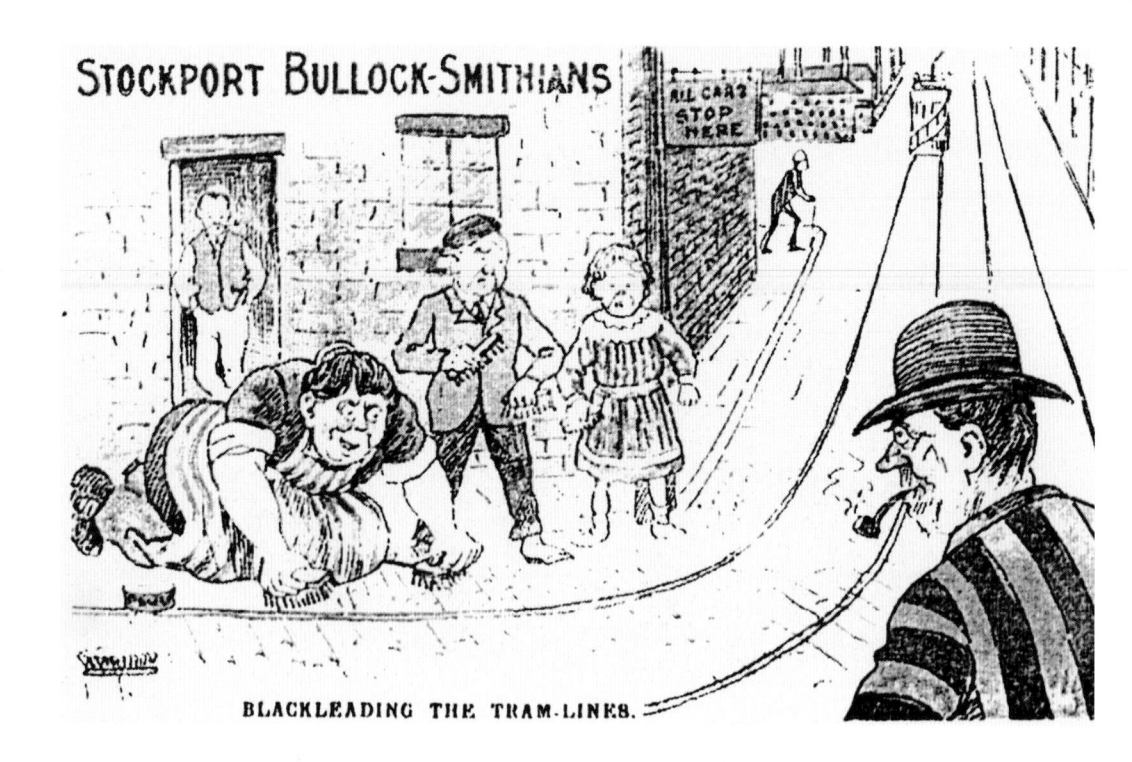

BLACKLEADING THE TRAM-LINES.

Above and below: Commemorating the demise of horse-drawn trams in Stockport.

In Affectionate Remembrance

OF THE

Hazel Grove Horse Cars

Which Succumbed to an
ELECTRIC SHOCK
JULY 5th, 1905.

After many years of faithful Service.

"GONE, BUT NOT FORGOTTEN."

Above: The first internal combustion engine bus ran on the Stockport to Offerton route in 1919 and had the registration number DB 1662. Here, bus No.102, registration number DB 1663, is seen with driver Albert E. Longden.

Below: In this photograph the same bus is seen at the Offerton terminus in 1921.

Right: This is an historic picture! Seen here in charge of tram No. 30 to Stockport are driver Albert E. Longden again, with conductress Millicent Preston. She was one of the last conductresses working at the end of the First World War. The photograph is dated 'end of 1919'.

Left: Here we see driver Batty and guard Johnson posing with their tram, with 'Stockport' just visible in its destination panel.

Like other transport undertakings, Stockport Corporation Transport Department ran illuminated trams to celebrate the Silver Jubilee of King George V and Queen Mary in 1935.

Above and next page above: The Transport Department also joined in the celebrations for the Coronation of King George VI and Queen Elizabeth in May 1937. The vehicles are a bus and tram although they are so heavily decorated you would hardly know it! Anything Blackpool can do … !

75

Left: Mr Edison, who was aged eighty-seven when this photograph was published in the local press in 1997, was believed to be the longest-serving surviving employee of Stockport Corporation's Transport Department. He worked for the undertaking for forty-six years, apart from war service spent on the Russian conveys, joining as a junior clerk in 1927 at the Heaton Lane Depot. He was the Chief Clerk at the new (1968) offices at Daw Bank when he retired in 1973.

LONGEST-SERVING BUSMAN: Sam Edison

five

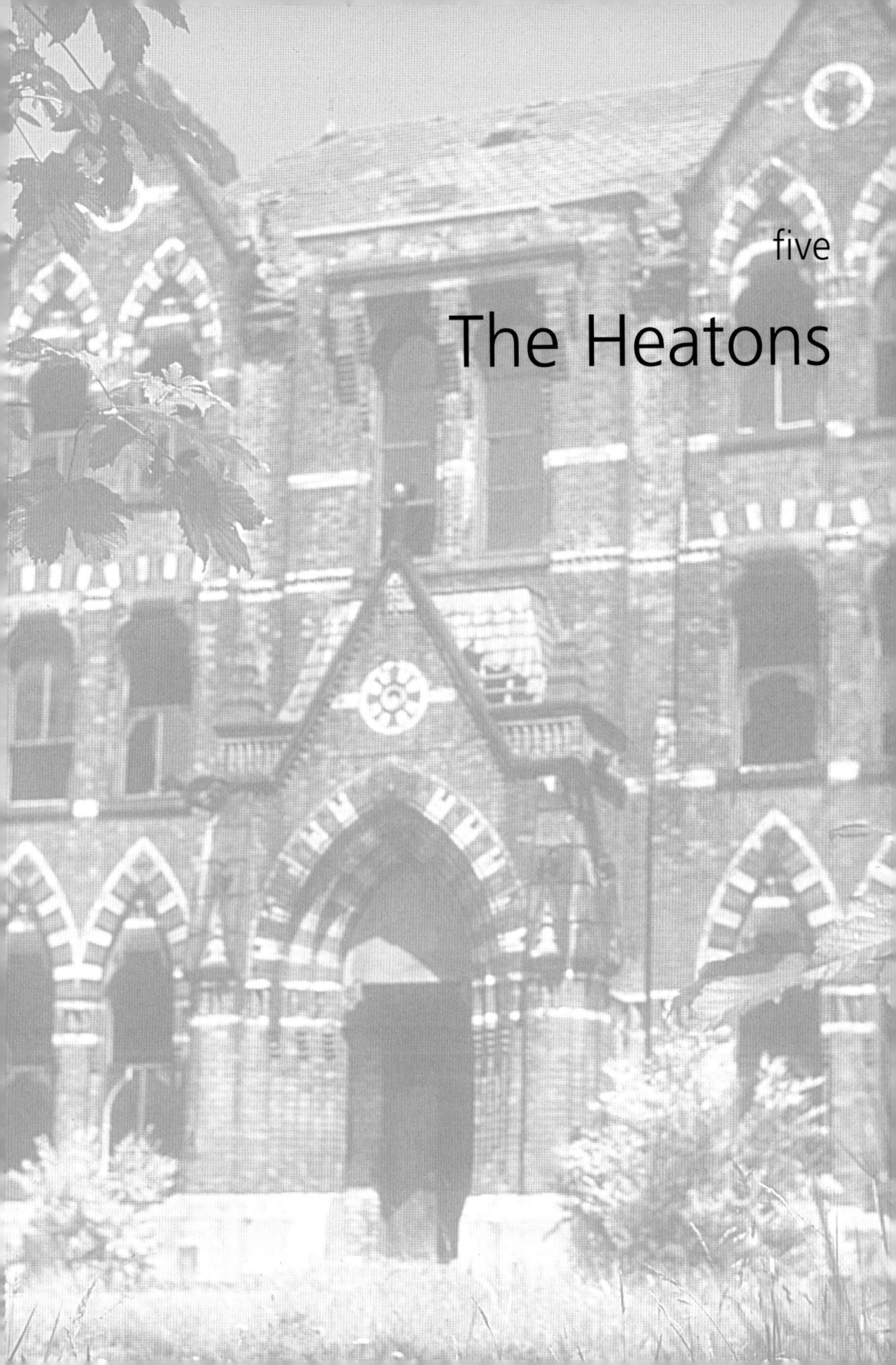

The Heatons

Over the years there have been a number of Heatons; perhaps today, largely because of its station on the line from Manchester to Stockport and beyond, the one most widely known is Heaton Chapel, whose station was established in 1852. But old records show that the area covered by 'The Heatons' has had a number of names, of which four currently survive: Heaton Chapel, Heaton Norris, Heaton Mersey and Heaton Moor, and further back in time we find Heaton Wood, Heaton Reddish and Heaton Moss and there was even a Heaton Strangeways! The Heatons became a part of the borough of Stockport relatively recently in historical terms, in 1913, though a part of Heaton Norris had been incorporated into Stockport in 1901. By then the area was partly industrial and partly residential, though its industrial base was to diminish as the century wore on, and the area is now largely residential. But it was not always so. In the introduction to her book *Old Heatonians: the Heatons in old photographs* (1977), Elizabeth Jones described it as 'a small area of moor, woodland and heath with fairly poor agricultural potential, sandwiched between the market town of Stockport to the south and the city of Manchester to the north…'.

Below: This rare and most interesting picture can be dated to the period 1894-1897. The tall figure in the carriage photographed by the George and Dragon, Heaton Chapel, is John Lacy (or Lacey) Hill, and the young boy next to him is his son, also John L. Hill, who was born in 1890. The lady in the rear is John's second wife, who died in 1897, with their youngest son Rowland, born 1894. Originally a farm built in 1824, the George and Dragon became a coaching inn and was rebuilt in its present form in about 1909.

Above left: John Lacey Hill, born in around 1858, died April 1900.

Above right: His second wife, Susannah Elliott, born in around 1859, died September 1897.

Below: The Hill family lived in Denby Lane for a time; this photograph dates from around 1910.

Above and below: These two photographs date from around 1895. Heaton Mersey Prize Band was formed in 1868, becoming Heaton Mersey Subscription Band in 1890 and then Heaton Mersey Prize Band. The first photograph shows the band outside Priestnall Hey, the home of Hans Renold. This may be the location of both these photographs.

80

Above: This picture shows the band as it was before 1890, when it adopted a more military-style uniform in place of the previous (as here) Sunday suit and bowler hat.

Below: The Barnes Home Boys Band, *c.* 1930.

Above and left: The Barnes Industrial Home in Heaton Mersey was a residential industrial school for boys, built with money left by Robert Barnes, a Manchester businessman. It had been opened by the Bishop of Manchester, Dr Frazer, on 21 August 1871. It cost £14,000 and was later extended; by the mid-1880s it had nearly 300 boys. The architect was Herbert Pinchbeck and the first master was Donald Ross, who died in 1909. The home was on Didsbury Road, before Bank Hall Road. At the rear of the site is now Barnes Avenue. In the mid-1950s it became offices for the National Coal Board and when they vacated it, in the later 1950s, it was demolished. These two photographs show the building as it was in July 1975. Robert Barnes, born in Bloom Street, Manchester, was a cotton spinner at Miles Platting and, later, in Jackson Street (off London Road). He was mayor of Manchester when it was created a city by Royal Charter on 29 March 1853. He died on Christmas Day 1871, aged 71, at his residence at Fallowfield. This was a house called 'Oakley', which by 1916 was the Oakley Private Hotel; it is now 188 Wilmslow Road and since the 1930s has been occupied by the Union of Shop, Distributive and Allied Workers (USDAW). A bust of Barnes which was in the grounds of his house was retrieved but has now gone and its present whereabouts are unknown.

Above: Gibson's Road in Heaton Mersey. The origin of the road's name is not known but in this early postcard it looks to be in a sylvan setting!

Right: It has not been possible to identify this street, but notice the cobbles (setts) – and the washing! This would have been a very common sight in the early years of the twentieth century.

Above and opposite above: Like everywhere else in May 1937 the people of Heaton Mersey celebrated the Coronation of King George VI and Queen Elizabeth. Bonfires were 'a must' on such occasions.

Opposite below: A Punch and Judy show would also have been a popular entertainment.

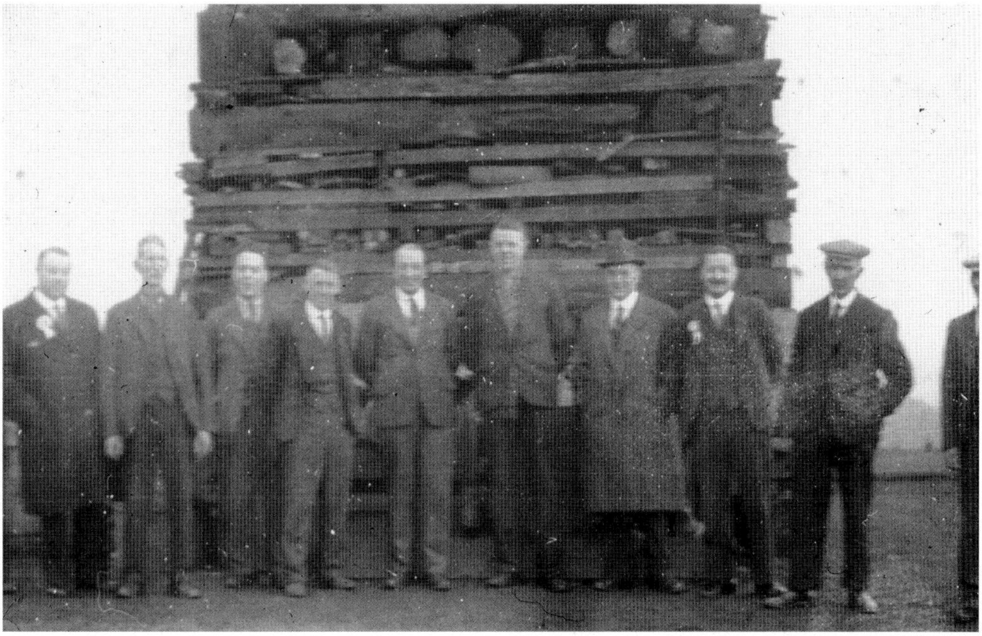

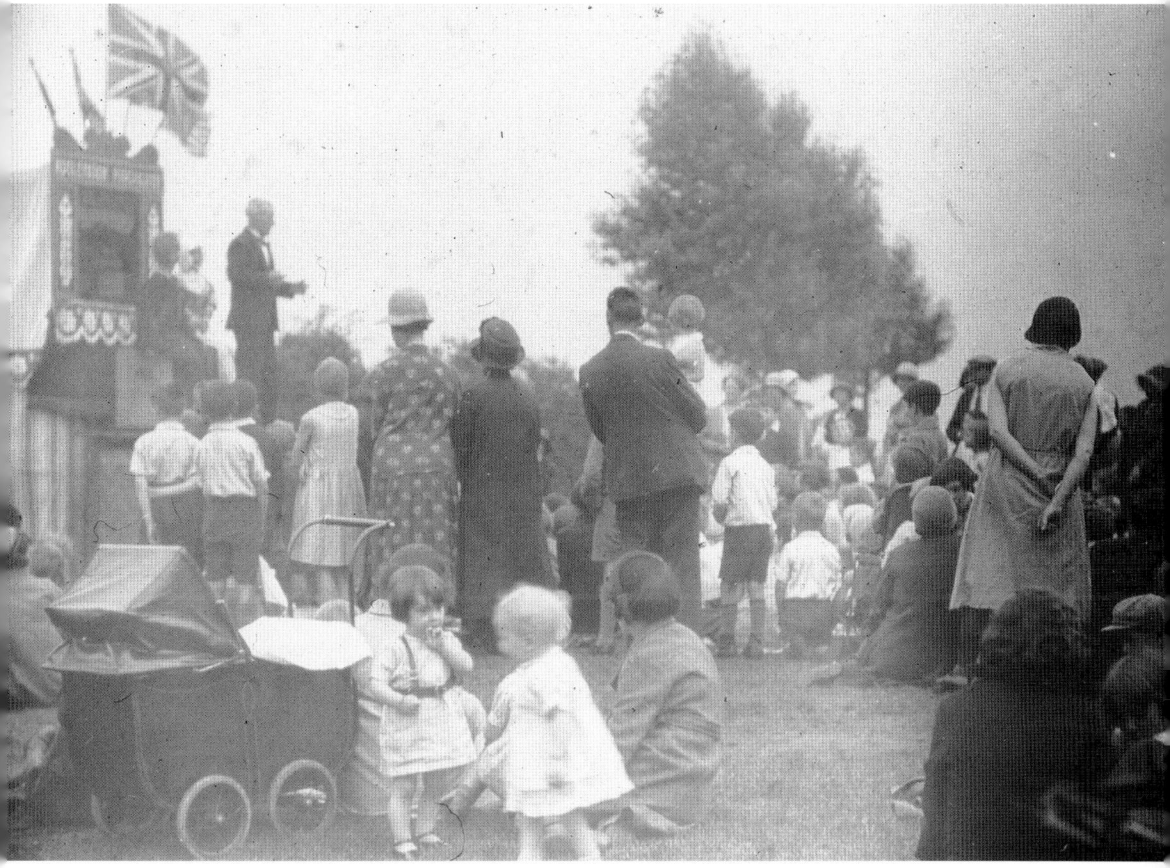

Above: The war memorial situated at the junction of Didsbury Road and Church Square was illuminated for the Coronation in 1937.

Opposite above and below: Heaton Mersey Congregational church was opened in 1840 and was twice extended. Here we see a group of ladies outside the church in about 1900 and in the other picture the old folks committee.

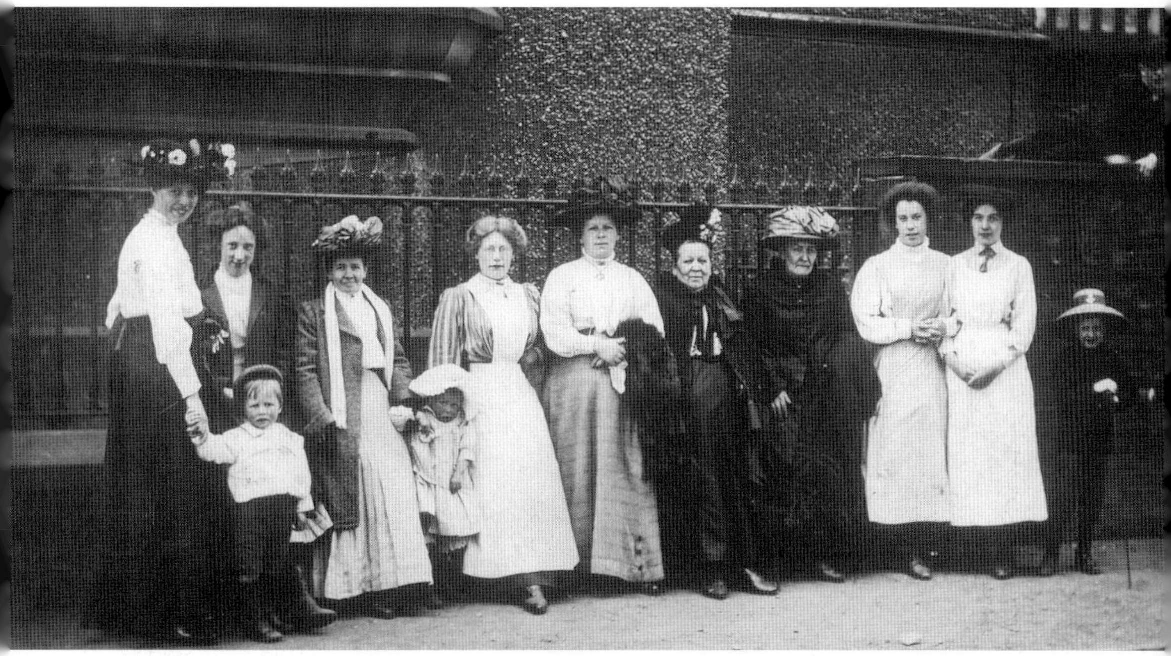

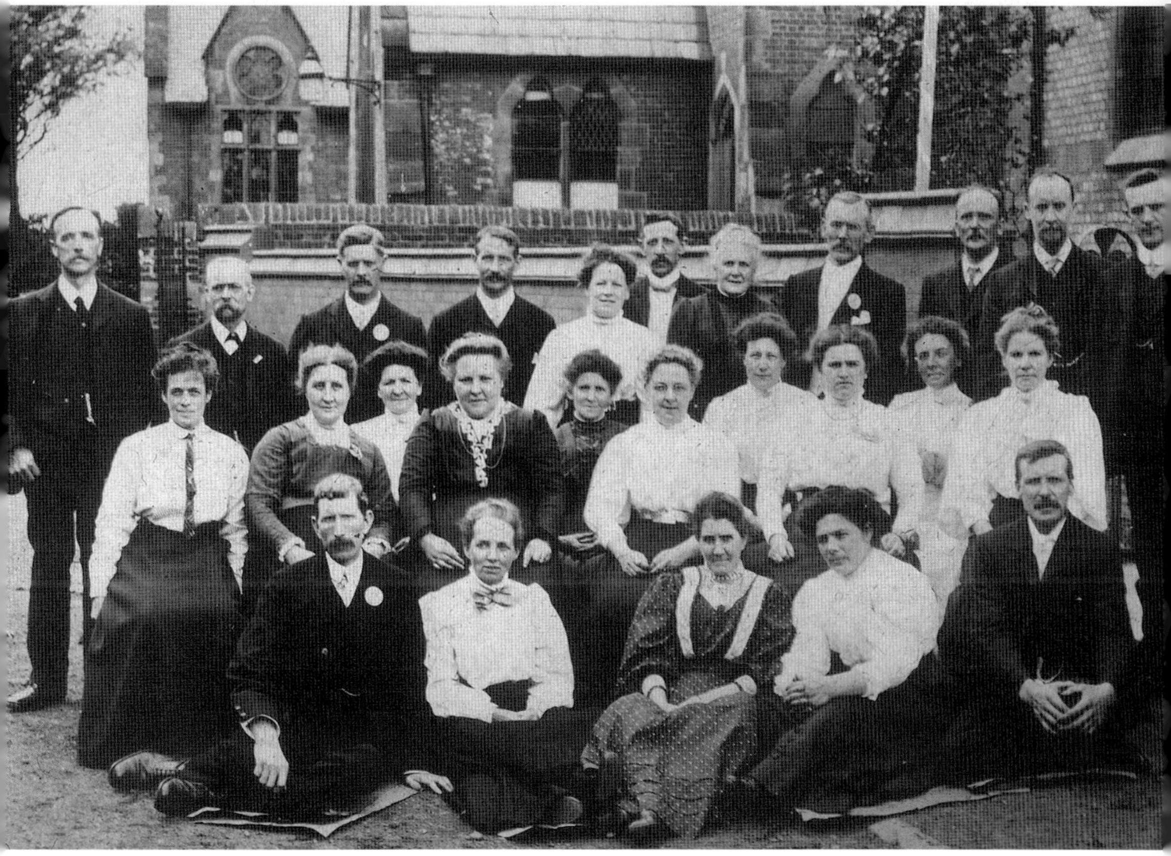

An early postcard view of Heaton Moor Road and Shaw Road, c. 1910.

Mauldeth Hall, seen here in a print from about 1880, was built in around 1830. The Ecclesiastical Commissioners purchased it in 1854 as a residence for the first Bishop of Manchester, James Prince Lee. In 1882 the Northern Counties Supplementary Hospital converted it into a home or hospital for people having incurable conditions.

six

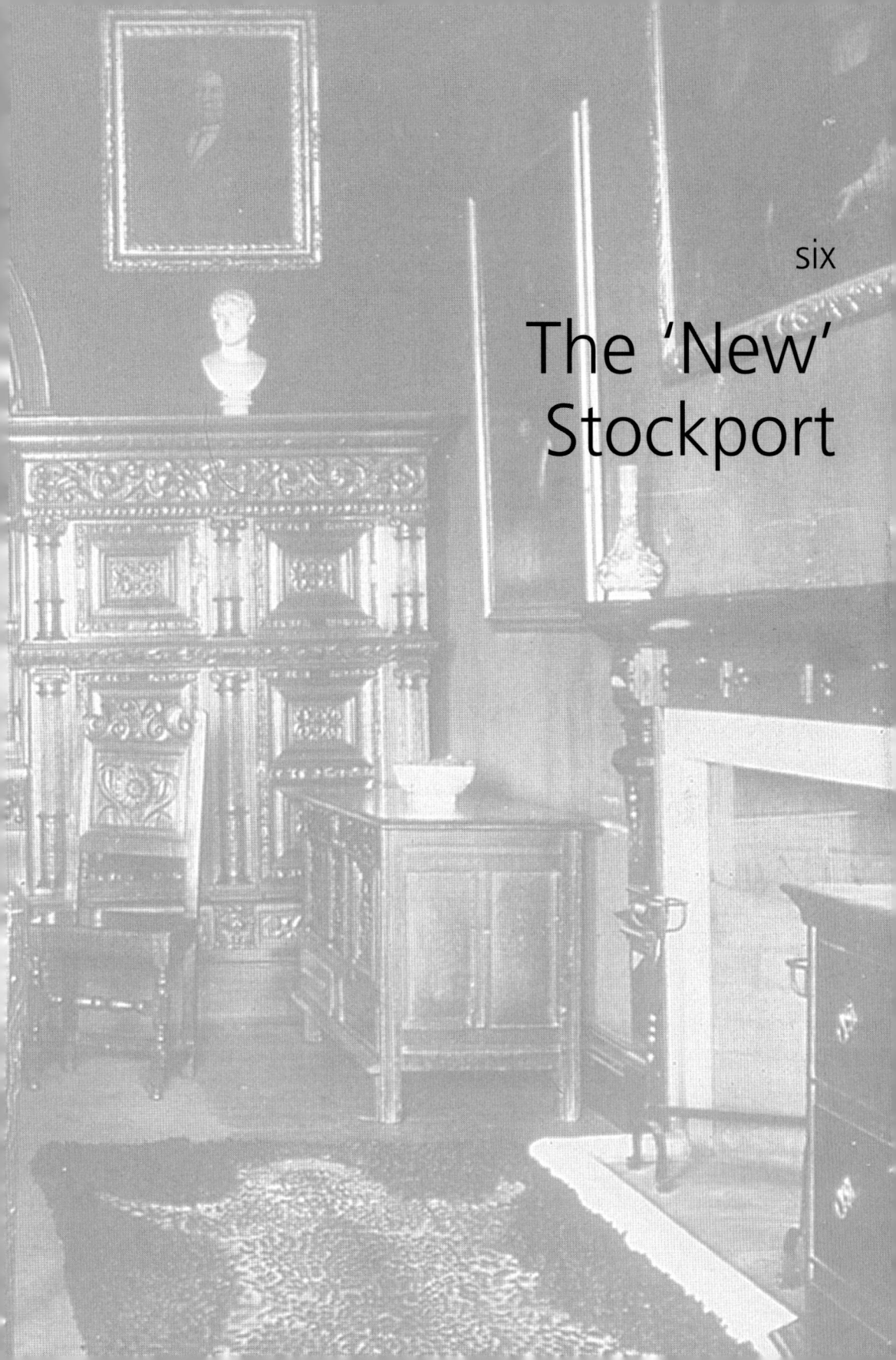

The 'New' Stockport

It can be argued with some justification that the five most important dates in the history of Stockport are: the granting of the charter in around 1220, by Sir Robert de Stokeport, by which he made the town a free borough; 1260, when the market charter was granted, enabling the lord of the manor to hold a Market every Friday, and an annual fair on St Wilfrid's Day (12 October) and the seven days afterwards; 1888, Stockport (including parts of adjacent townships) was created a county borough; 1901, by the Stockport Extension Order, other townships were included within the county borough. Finally, in the 1974 Local Government Act other areas of Cheshire were transferred to Stockport, to form a new local authority, the Stockport Metropolitan Borough. This section reflects this enlarged borough of Stockport.

BRAMHALL LANE, BRAMHALL.

Bramhall Lane extends from its junction with Buxton Road (A6) at Heaviley, by the Blossoms Hotel, into the centre of Bramhall village. In this image from a postcard of around 1910 the rural nature of the area a century ago is a striking feature. The railway had arrived in 1845 and commuters were already being encouraged to live in the area.

90

Above: A delightful scene in Moss Lane, Bramhall, from an early coloured postcard.

Right: Situated on Bramhall Lane South, just across the road from Bramhall Library, these three cottages, collectively known as Benja Fold, are a quiet oasis in the busy village. The area is named after Benjamin Birchenough, who owned the land in the eighteenth century. The picture is from an early postcard. Two of the three cottages are still thatched.

BRAMHALL GREEN.

Above: Bramhall Green, looking towards Bridge Lane, c. 1905. Bramhall developed from a number of scattered hamlets, of which Bramhall Green was one. How peaceful it was a century ago: no traffic, no large roundabout or intrusive road signs!

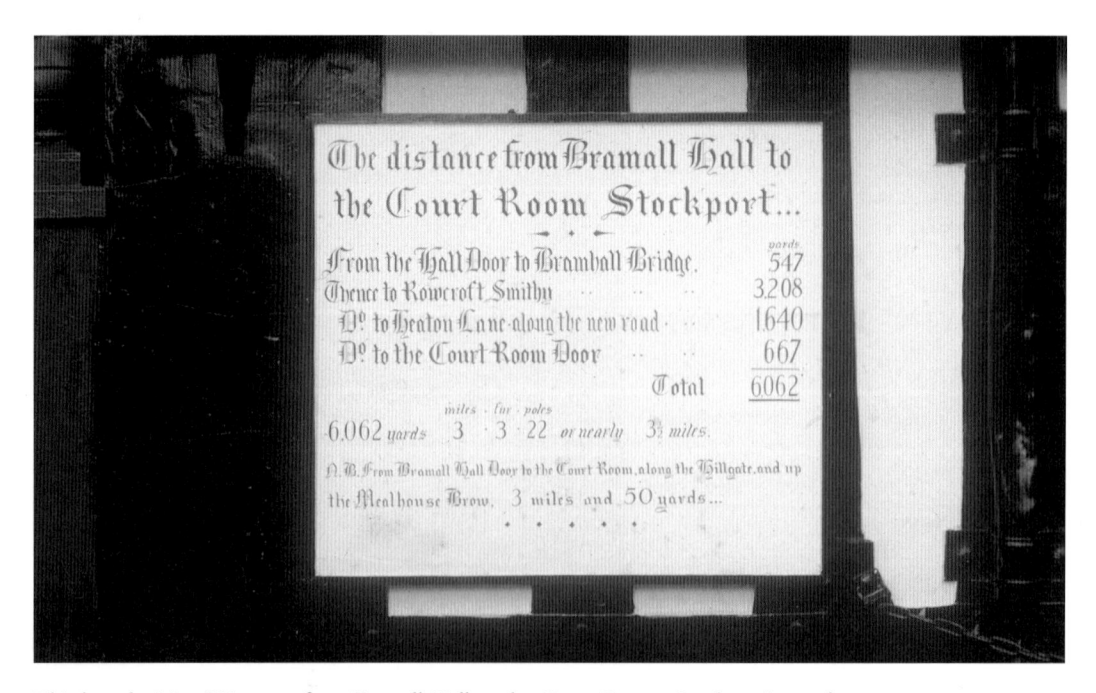

The distance from Bramall Hall to the Court Room Stockport...

	yards
From the Hall Door to Bramall Bridge.	547
Thence to Rowcroft Smithy	3,208
D? to Heaton Lane along the new road	1,640
D? to the Court Room Door	667
Total	6,062

miles · fur · poles
6,062 yards   3 · 3 · 22   or nearly 3½ miles.

N.B. From Bramall Hall Door to the Court Room, along the Hillgate, and up the Mealhouse Brow, 3 miles and 50 yards...

This board, giving 'Distances from Bramall Hall to the Court Room, Stockport', was for many years a feature of the courtyard at the Hall. It is seen here as it was in June 1969.

92

The origins of Bramall Hall can be traced back to around 1370. It was the home of the Davenport family until 1877 when it was bought by the Freeholders Company of Manchester. In 1882 it was purchased by Charles Henry Nevill, a calico printer, who had a great interest in architecture and history. As the Hall by then was in a poor state of repair, he immediately began a programme of restoration. He retained all the best features from several different periods, and incorporated many Victorian features to make it into a comfortable home. The Nevill family sold it in 1925 to John Henry Davies, a local brewer; he died in 1927, his widow staying on until 1935. Today it is in the ownership of the local authority. Here, in June/July 1993, we see staff at the Hall taking part in a Victorian 'Living History' event. Left to right: Kate Allies, Wendy Robinson, Bill Hawksworth, Eileen Garratt, Judy Oldroyd and Hazel Fuller.

Above: In 1935 Mrs Amy Davies sold the Hall to the Hazel Grove & Bramhall Urban District Council, in whose care it remained until 1974, when the UDC was absorbed into Stockport Metropolitan Borough under local government reorganisation. The UDC's information board, seen here as it looked in June 1969, was situated just off Bramhall Green, at the entrance to the driveway.

Opposite below and right: Halfway along the driveway the visitor is rewarded with these views of the Hall, taken in June 1969. I am assured that subtle changes have taken place in the foliage since then!

In 1991 Mrs Garbe in Florida wrote to say she had a grandfather clock in her possession which had a note inside it saying that it had originally stood at the foot of the stairs at the Hall. If a means could be found of transporting it, she would donate it back to its original home. Here Vicki Dawson, then the Hall Manager, and Donald Outhwaite, the late Chairman of the Friends of Bramall Hall, celebrate its return in 1992.

Arden Hall, Bredbury, also known as Harden Hall, was formerly the residence of the Ardern(e) family. The building dates from the late sixteenth century – it was rebuilt in stone in 1597-1602. This illustration is from an early coloured postcard; today some remains may still be seen. Ralph Arderne, with troops raised from his own tenantry, supported the Parliamentary garrison at Manchester in 1642. The town was besieged by Royalist forces under Lord Strange, who became the 7th Earl of Derby during the unsuccessful siege due to the death of his father.

This print, from Heginbotham's *Stockport: Ancient and Modern*, shows Bredbury Hall as it looked in 1810. It is a copy of a drawing made early in the nineteenth century by William Shuttleworth of Stockport,

When the first Harrytown Hall at Bredbury was built is not known, but it was owned by Henry Collier in 1580. In 1600 it was bought by John Bruckshawe. It was rebuilt in 1671 by John and Sarah Bruckshawe: this date and the initials IBS are carved above one of the entrances. It was sold to William Walton in 1860. From 1912 to 1949 it was a school run by the Sisters of Evron, and between 1949 and 1983 it was a grammar school and then Harrytown High School Convent. From 1982 to 1983 that section of the Hall not being used by the school was refurbished into luxury flats. This postcard view dates from around 1910.

A record of the visit of HRH the Princess Royal, on Monday 26 July 1948, in connection with the Cheadle and Gatley District YMCA appeal. Seen with Her Royal Highness is the Chairman of Cheadle and Gatley UDC, Councillor H. Howard Robinson, JP, CC. Others to be seen are, left to right: Mr J. Huxley (UDC Parks Superintendent), Councillor Harry Briggs (Chairman, Parks Committee) and Mr Wilson Downs (UDC Treasurer). The lady talking to Mr Downs is thought to be one of HRH's ladies-in-waiting.

Above: Mellor Road in Cheadle Hulme was originally called Mellor Street, changing its name about 1905 or 1906. In the middle distance a lone female cyclist has the road temporarily to herself. The awnings over the shop proclaim 'W.H. Dupoy & Co. Ltd'

Methodism in Cheadle Hulme can be dated to 1787 when the Stockport Circuit Membership Roll for that year lists eighteen members at Gill Bent and eight at Cheadle Hulme. The first meeting place was 'The Upper Room' above three cottages, Nos 57-61 Station Road. The first chapel was on the site of Nos 97 and 99 Station Road. The second chapel, designed by J.S. Whittington of Manchester, opened in 1884. It was severely damaged by fire on the evening of Tuesday 26 February 1963. This photograph states that this is 'the site for the new Methodist Church'. This new church was opened and dedicated on Saturday 2 March 1968 at 3 p.m.; the architect was Charles Brown (Denys Hinton and Partners).

Right: South Park, on Grove Lane in 1974. This open space has been much-loved by local residents and others for years. The slide was a popular feature.

Opposite below: This photograph, an early postcard view of Church Road, formerly Church Lane, in Cheadle Hulme, conveys very much a village atmosphere in contrast to the present busy road. The National School beyond the shops opened in 1873 and was demolished in 1973. All Saints church is hidden from view beyond the school except for the porch roof.

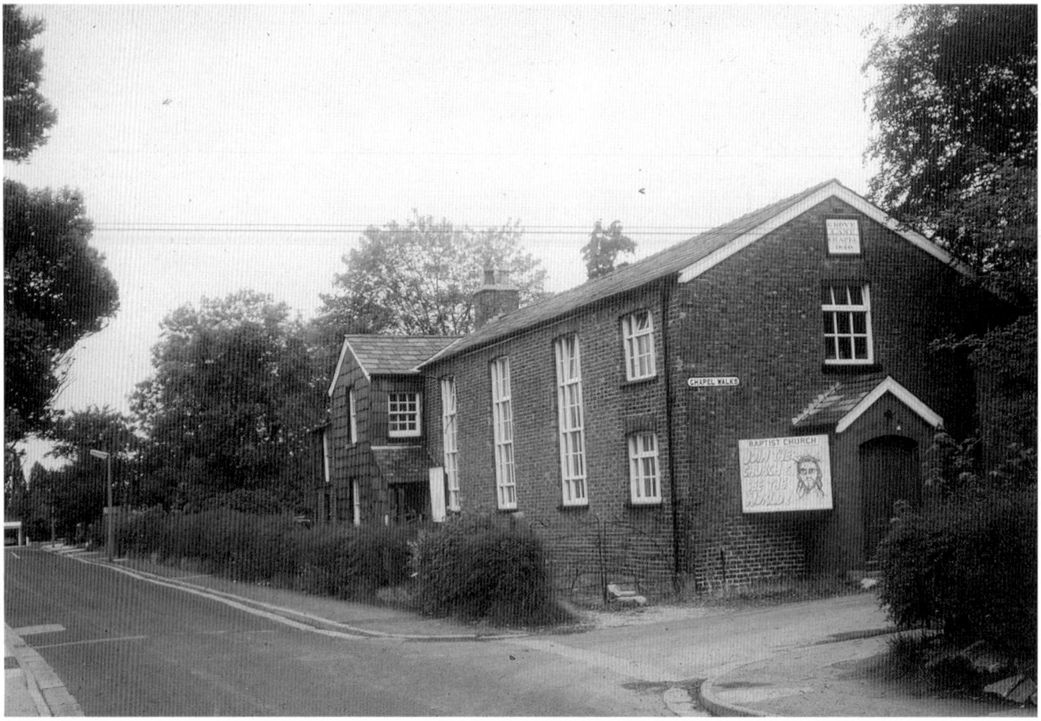
CHAPEL WALKS
BAPTIST CHURCH

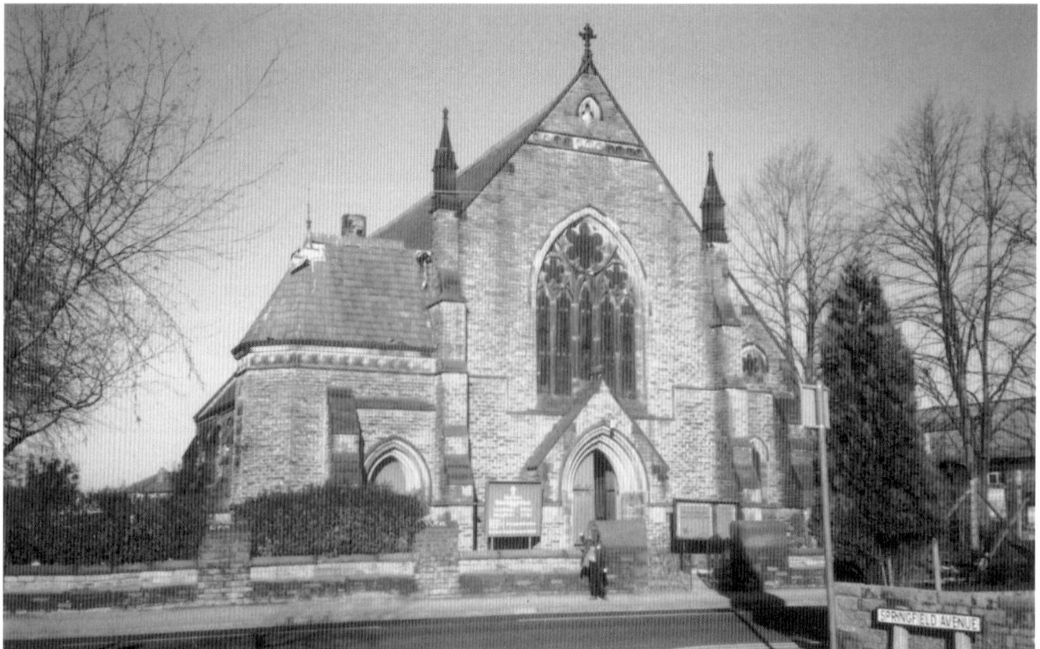
SPRINGFIELD AVENUE

The Carrs at Gatley is a former refuse tip which was re-seeded in the 1930s. It has recently been declared an official English Nature Local Nature Reserve and consists of nineteen acres of woodland, scrubland and grassland and four acres of willow carr swamp with two ponds. In this photograph from the early years of the last century we see the rural nature of the area. The Alder Leaf Beetle, previously thought to be extinct in this country, was discovered here in 2004.

Opposite above: Grove Lane Baptist Chapel, Cheadle Hulme, was actually on the corner of Pingate Lane (which joins Grove Lane) and Chapel Walks and was built in 1840, paid for by William Fowden, then aged 56, who was born in a nearby farmhouse. Fowden was concerned for the welfare of the people of this area. Not content with building the chapel, he also paid for the Grove Lane Day and Sunday School across the road on Grove Lane in 1846; this building is now used by David Bratt and Sons (Haulage) Ltd. Grove Lane Baptist church, being deemed unsafe, was demolished in 1997, having been replaced by a smaller building erected within its land; the site of the original building is now a landscaped car park for the new chapel. This photograph, from July 1975, shows the view from Pingate Lane, with Chapel Walks on the right.

Opposite below: The United Reformed church on Commercial Road, Hazel Grove, seen here in 1986 prior to demolition in the same year.

Two unidentified Hazel Grove batsmen about to go out and face the Stockport Sunday School bowlers at Wesley Park in July 1951. The Sunday School won by three wickets.

The Peak Forest Canal, authorised in 1794, ran from Dukinfield to Buxworth in Derbyshire to carry limestone from quarries at Dove Holes near Buxton. The locks at Marple extend for 1.5 kilometres and link the two levels of the canal. The canal opened in 1800 but the flight of sixteen locks, raising or lowering barges the 60 metres between the two levels, was not completed until 1804. Until then goods were transferred between the barges by means of a tramroad. This picture is from an early postcard.

Following pages: In 1606 the Marple Estate was purchased by Henry Bradshaw, who rebuilt the house in stone in the 1650s; it had thirteen hearths in the 1664 Hearth Tax Returns. He has the distinction of being the grandfather of both the Parliamentarian officer Henry Bradshaw and of John Bradshaw, the first signatory on the death warrant of Charles I. The Bradshaws were a wealthy family and the principal family in the area in the seventeenth century. The owner in 1950, Richard Isherwood, the brother of Christopher, the novelist, offered the Hall to Marple Urban District Council; this was declined due to the high cost of necessary repairs and it was demolished in 1959. In the third of these exterior views may be seen the stables and clock tower, while the interior views, of the dining room and the drawing room, give some idea of its former splendour.

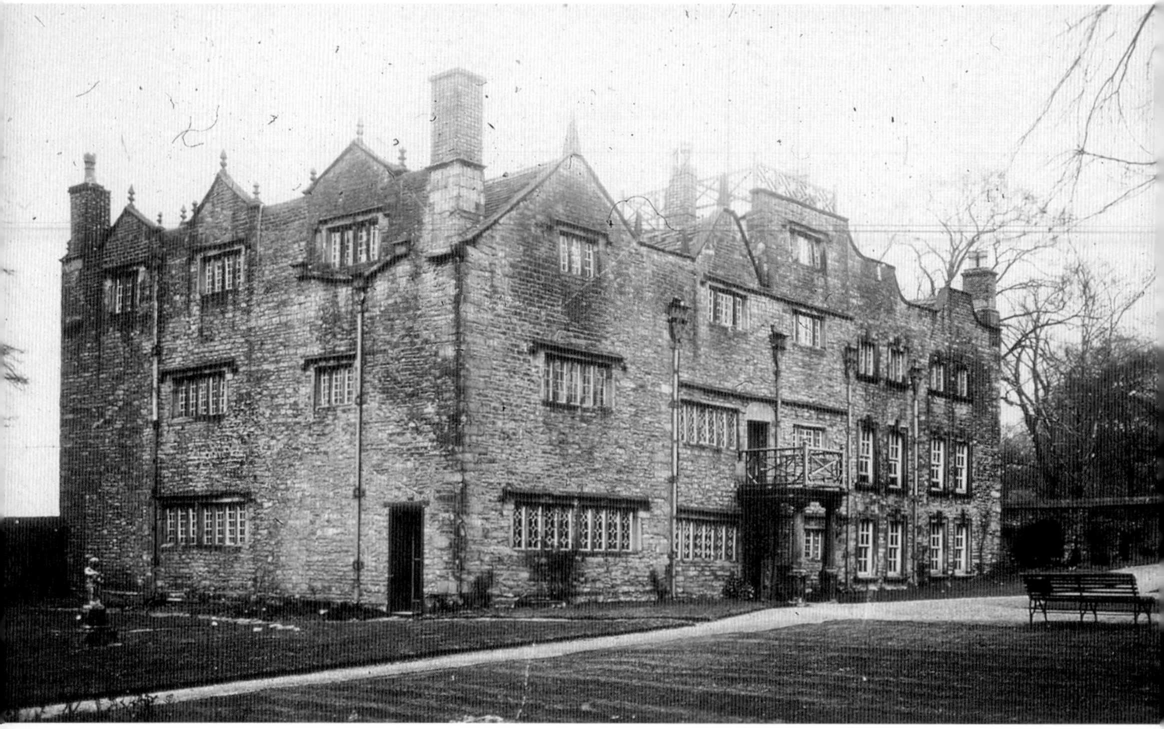

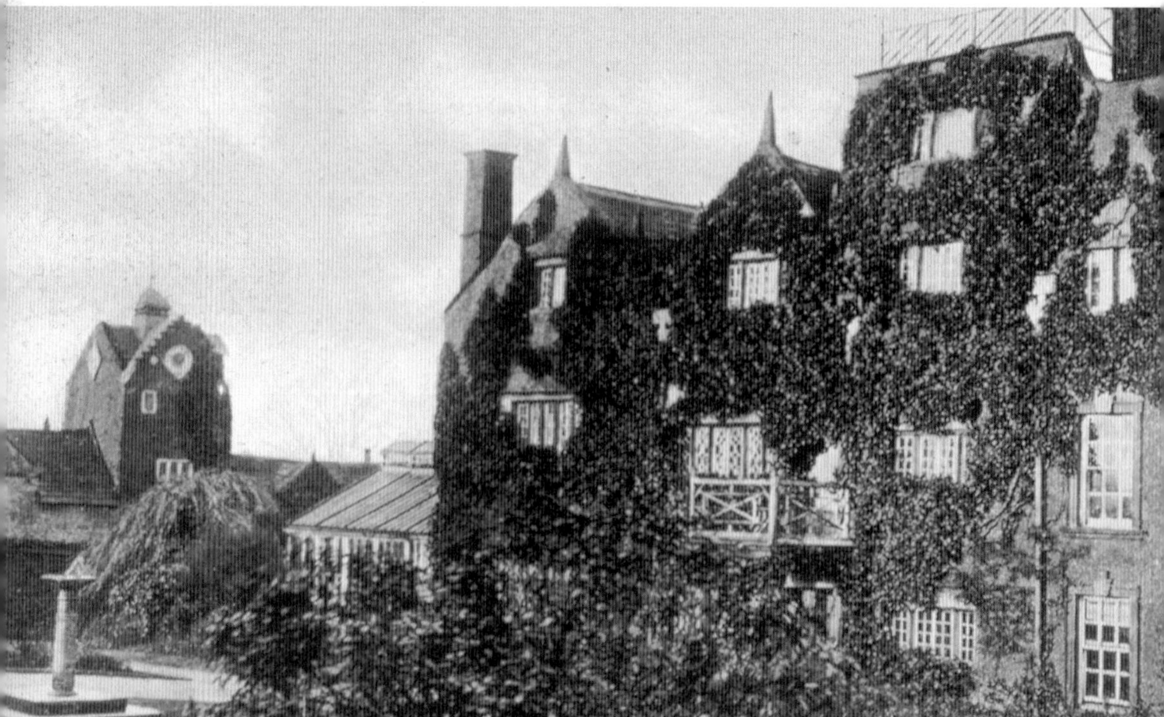

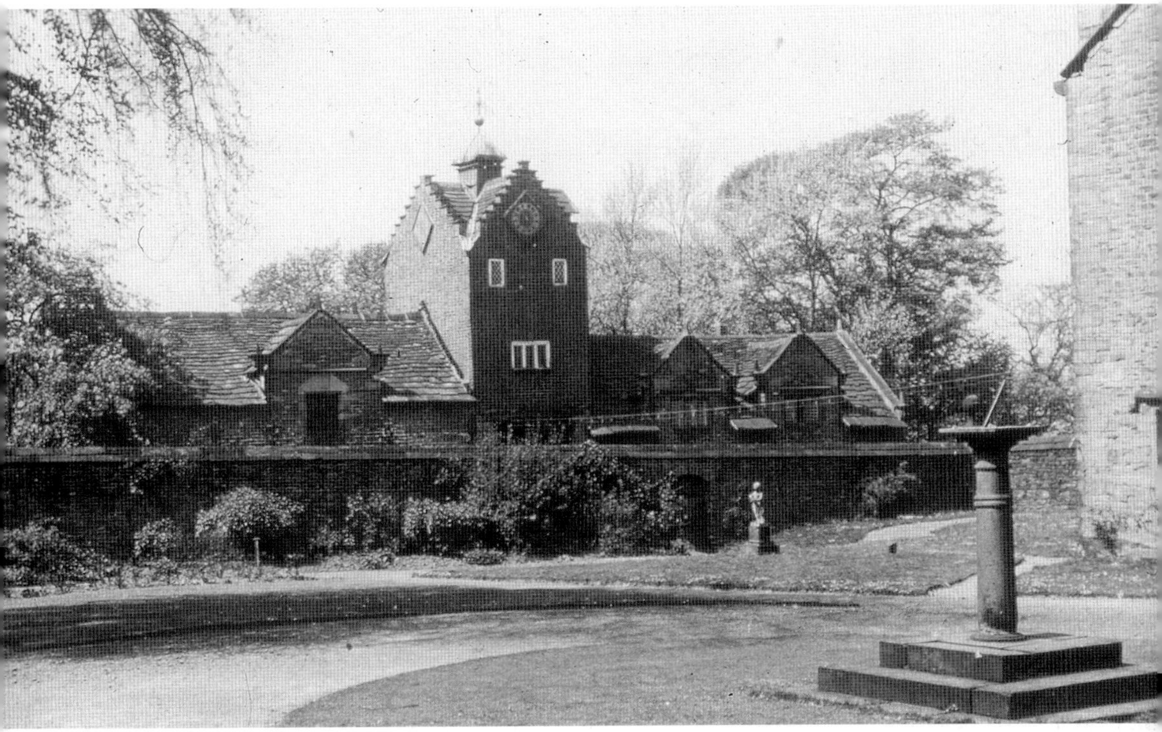

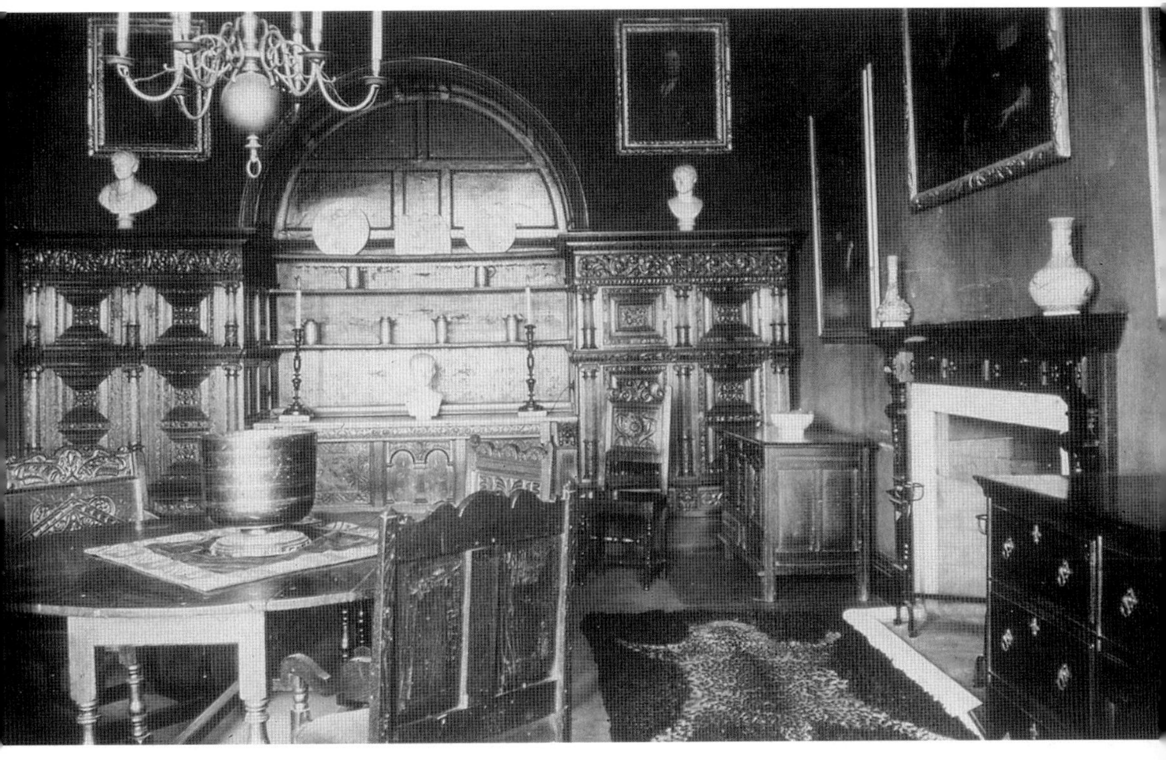

Marple Hall view of the drawing room.

Looking across an early bridge over the River Goyt towards Brabyns Brow, the steepness of the hill and the dangerous bend are somewhat obscured by the angle of the camera. The house in the centre of this early postcard view belonged to Dr Hibbert. This, and the cottages to the left of the bridge, were demolished in 1930 when the road and bridge were widened.

Right: Even today Middlewood preserves the rural character recorded in this early coloured postcard from, probably, just before the First World War.

Below and overleaf: British Aerospace Woodford is situated on the southern boundary of the Metropolitan Borough. It covered 450 acres and there was a large assembly shop, flight sheds and a main runway, 7,500ft long. The Air Show was a much-loved charity event which attracted enthusiasts from a wide area. These photographs are from the show held on Saturday 30 June 1984. We see, respectively, a Mustang, a Harrier demonstrating its manoeuvrability and an Avro Vulcan, like those used in the Falklands War of 1982.

107

seven

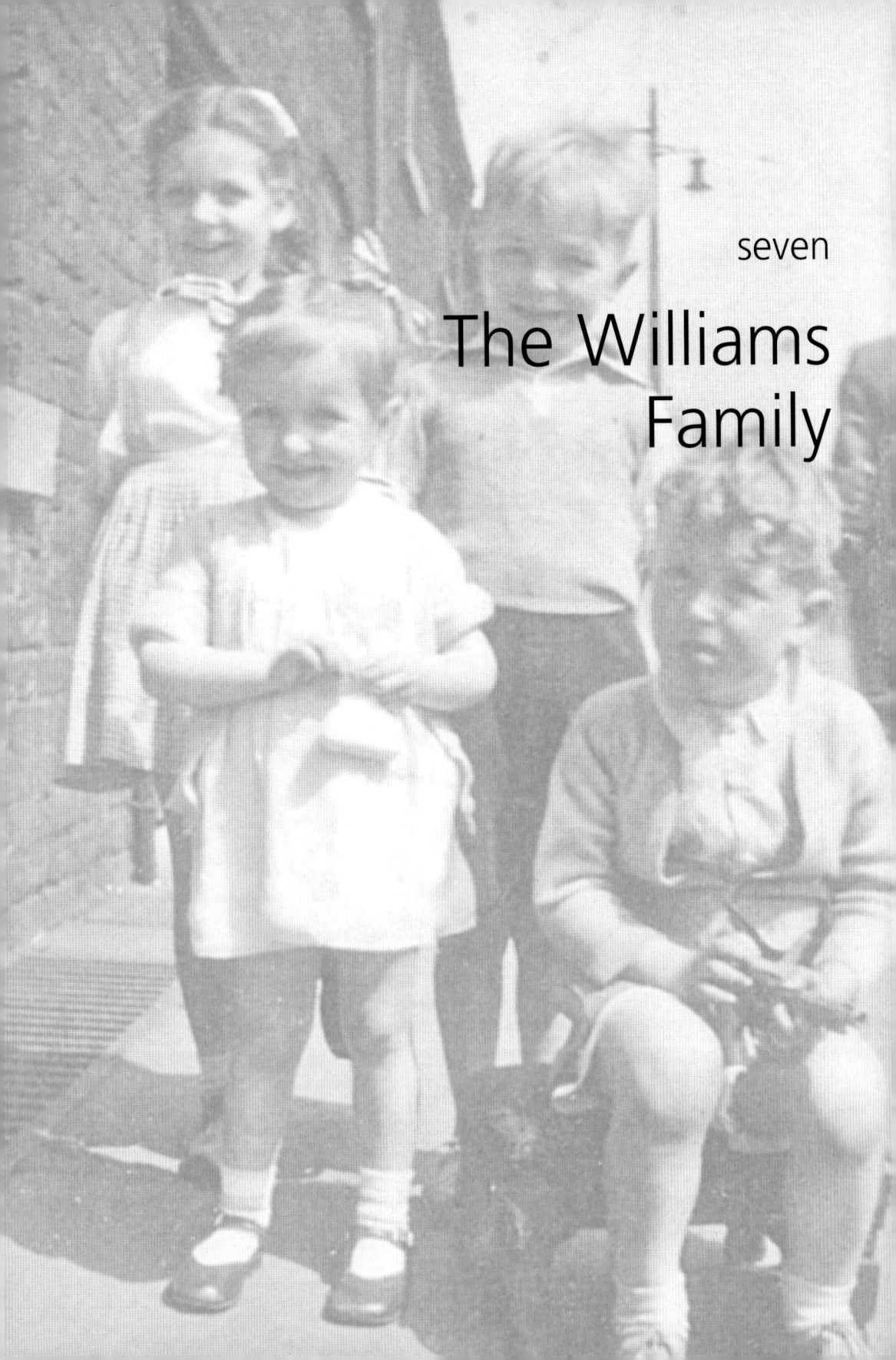

The Williams Family

Interest in family history has never been greater and no doubt it will be further stimulated by programmes on television, like the BBC's *Who do you think you are?* Searching for, collecting and interpreting old family photographs has become a growth industry. But although many families in the early days of photography could not afford to have their photograph taken, as the industry developed and as the equipment became less expensive, more and more people visited photographic studios or were able to buy a camera with which to take images of their own family. In the beginning these tended to be of the formal portrait type, but as films and lenses were developed to record moving images, so people were photographed at work, at play, in the home – indeed, anywhere. What is tragic is that sometimes when clearing out, perhaps after a death or when a family member has left home, so many of these precious documents are destroyed.

When Shirley McKenna and I compiled an earlier book of Stockport photographs we included a number of photographs from the Williams family collection. Linda Williams, now Linda Lewis, formerly of Stockport but now living in Australia, was helpful in making her family photographs available to us. It is therefore pleasing for me to record my thanks to her and her family for making even more images available for this book. I think this is a 'first' and I hope that you, the reader, will agree that if these pictures were distributed under other headings in the book, their impact would have been diminished.

Opposite: The family are dressed ready for a fancy dress ball, *c.* 1900.

Left: Linda's ancestors, Joseph Percy Clarke and Ellen Maria Clarke and their family lived on Hillgate.

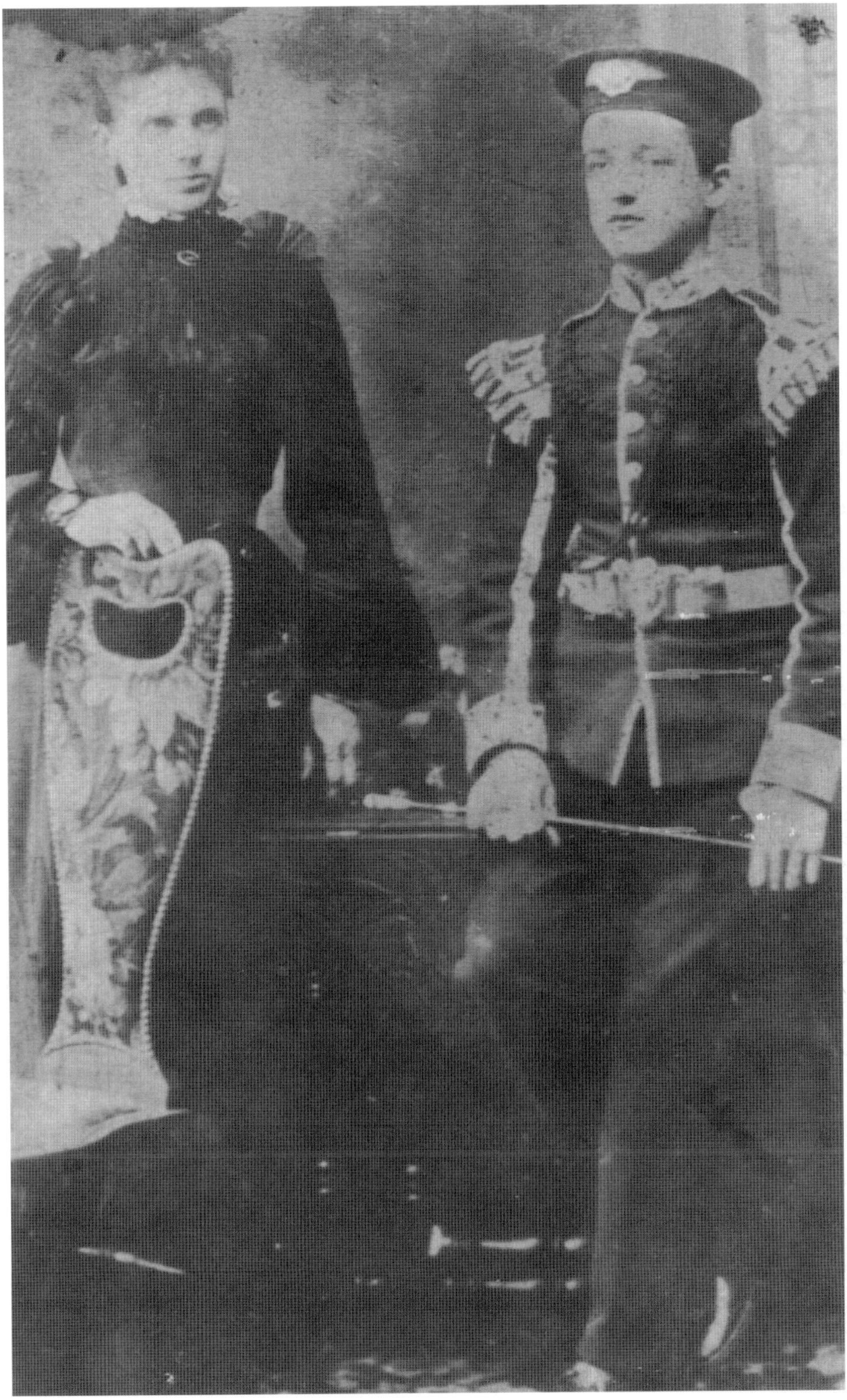

Above left and right: Their son Ean Mackenzie Clarke is seen here first at a military camp and, secondly, in private life. He was popularly called 'Dapper' and it is not difficult to see why!

Above: Thomas Markham with his grandchildren Ian and Linda Williams.

Opposite below: Thomas and Margaret Markham seen on 16 December 1947, at their home, 33 Aberdeen Crescent, Edgeley.

Left and below: Here we see the Markham twins, Ivy and Arthur, in the garden playing 'Nippy and Bob' with sister Edith.

Above: Portwood schoolchildren, with the twins Arthur (bottom row, first left) and Ivy (second row, third right), *c.* 1930.

Right: Edith Williams, mother of Ian and Linda, with her great-nephew Wayne.

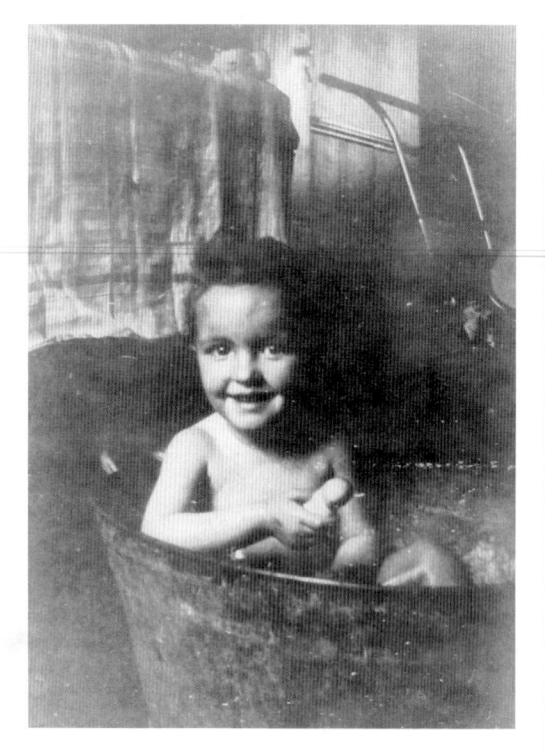

This page: For a time the Williams family lived at 94 Brinksway and these three scenes are from that period. The house was a two-up and two-down with an outside toilet and definitely no bathroom! In the first photograph, Linda takes a bath, then Ian and Linda are seen with two friends outside the house, then finally Linda, outside the house, is ready for a Sunday School walk – perhaps after that bath!

Right: John Williams, Ian and Linda's father, playing bowls in Alexandra Park on 21 July 1951.

Below: Brinksway Sunday School parade or fête, *c.* 1951.

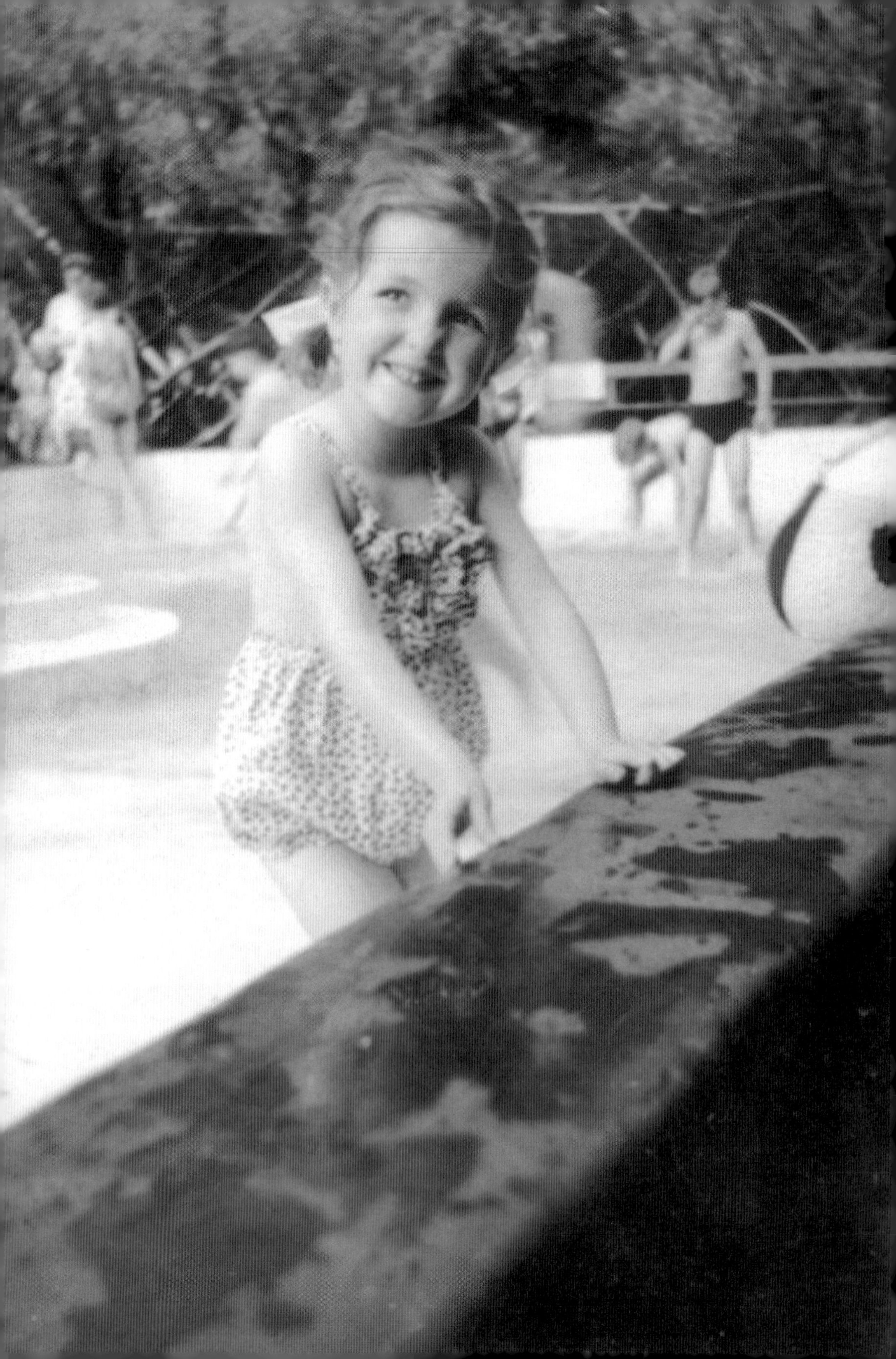

Hollywood Park School, built in 1906, was opened on 26 August 1907 and provided for 700 children. It is situated in Hardman Street at the foot of Hollywood Park. It operated as a school until 11 April 1915 when it became a military hospital during the First World War, and was a school again from 8 September 1919 until 1979-1980. It now houses the Hollywood Park Combined Nursery Centre, the Stockport Learning Centre, the Stockport English Language (ESOL) Unit, and Stepping Stones. Nearby is the Park View Resources Centre. This class photograph of eight-year olds from Hollywood Park School is thought to be from June 1952. The pupils are, left to right, back row: Ian Williams, Eric Robinson, David Pearson, Brian Turner, Kenneth Shaw. Middle row: Eric Warburton, Joe Mackmarn, Peter Warhurst, Irene Hiles, Maureen Kitchen, Jack Hargreaves, David Lester and Harry Pegg. Front row: Pauline Maydew, Joyce Williamson, Jean Benthom, Maureen Dyce, Jean Cotral, Enid Wilson, Sheila Ryan and Carol Croft.

Opposite: The Blue Lagoon was an open-air swimming pool at Mile End and except for one near Birmingham, it was the largest pool of this kind outside the London area. The pool was 120ft long and 60ft wide and held 30,000 gallons of water. It opened on Saturday 11 July 1936 and cost £8,000. Bathers paid 1s on weekdays and Sunday mornings up to 10.30 a.m., after which time it was 1s 6d (spectators paid 6d). It was a popular venue for children, especially Linda, as we see here. It closed in 1965.

Brindale Primary School, 1953. With teacher Miss Maher are, back row: Ian Diver, first left, David Hammond, third left, and Robert Henshaw, second right. Second row: Janice Garrett, third left, and Pauline Beeston, fourth left. Third row: Barbara Etchells, third left. Front row: Linda Williams, fourth right, Glenda Jackson, second right, and Norma Derbyshire, first right.

The same school a year later, and some of the same people. Back row: Hayden Hoole, third left, David Hammond, third right, Robert Henshaw, second right. Second row from top: Lynda Johnson, first left, Barbara Etchells, second right, Pauline Beeston, first right. Third row: Norma Derbyshire, second right. Front row: Janice Garrett (second left), Linda Williams, third right, Glenda Jackson, first right. Front row: Paul Holt, third left, Patrick Kitchen, third right, Ian Diver, second right.

Brindale Primary School Christmas Concert, c. 1954. The dancers (middle row) are Linda Williams and Pauline Beeston. David Hammond is second left on the top row and Carol Flowers is second right on the bottom row.

What a sporty lot of girls! This is Offerton Secondary Modern School for Girls, and this is the Rounders Team, c. 1959. Linda Williams is sitting first right.

Left: St Andrew's Pipe Band was founded in 1953-54 and disbanded in 1964. It was Stockport's only pipe band. In 1962 they played in the World Pipe Band Championship in Dumfries and in 1961 the drum section became the All-England 4th Grade Champions at Blackpool. Ian and Linda Williams, piper and dancer for the band, in the back garden of 58 Brindale Road, Brinnington, *c.* 1956.

Below: St Andrews Pipe Band Highland Dancers in around 1956. Back row: Irene Dan second left. Middle row: Lynda Johnson, Doreen Higginbottom, -?- , Betty Thompson, -?- . Front row: Joan Thompson, Lyn Jones, -?- , Mavis Thompson, -?- , Linda Williams.

Right: Ian Williams outside Palatine House, Edgeley, in the uniform of the Prince Charles Edward Pipe Band from Manchester, *c.* 1964. Most of the St Andrews Band members transferred to this band after their own band was disbanded.

Below: St Andrews Pipe Band of Stockport performing at Mirrlees Sports Day, *c.* 1958.

The St Andrews dancers (Linda Williams, centre) at Brindale Primary School Carnival performing the sword dance, *c.* 1956.

The St Andrews Pipe Band provides a Guard of Honour at the wedding of Linda Williams and Barry Lewis at St Matthew's church, Edgeley, on 7 August 1965. The pipers are, left to right: Peter Duncan, Brian Jones, Harold Jones and Neville Melling.

eight

And Finally…

A selection of four postcards of Stockport for your enjoyment!

What they say about Stockport.

Greetings from Stockport.

A postcard with five views.

A postcard with five views.

Other local titles published by Tempus

Gorton: The Second Selection
JILL CRONIN AND FRANK RHODES

A fascinating collection of over 220 archive photographs taking a look at some of the changes in leisure, housing, business and industry which have taken place over the last century in Gorton. A nostalgic look back at the pubs, cinemas, churches and schools that have changed over the years, including poignant photographs of VE Day street party celebrations. Each picture is supported by a wealth of historical detail sure to appeal to all who know, or have known, Gorton.

0 7524 2669 9

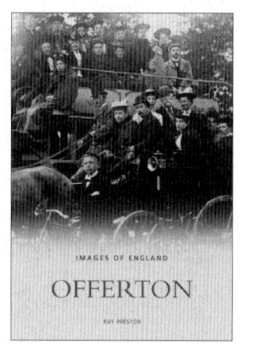

Offerton
RAY PRESTON

Originally a network of farms and mills to the west of the River Goyt, a close local community grew as the village developed and spread. Collecting together over 200 old photographs, this book describes Offerton through the ages, from Roman river crossings to twentieth-century conservation initiatives. A Nostalgic record of life in Offerton, this valuable pictorial history will be of interest to anyone who has lived here, and will provide others with an understanding of how the village has evolved.

0 7524 3450 0

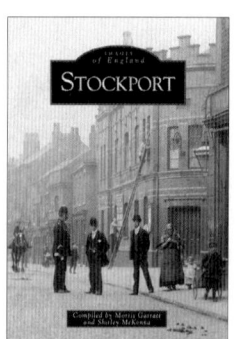

Stockport
MORRIS GARRATT AND SHIRLEY MCKENNA

This collection of 220 photographs and illustrations comes from a wide variety of sources and many of them have never been previously published. Covering Stockport town centre, Vernon Park, Portwood and Brinnington, Tiviot Dale and Lancashire Hill, the Heatons and Edgeley, Cale Green and Davenport, this volume will re-awaken memories among older residents, while showing the younger and newer residents the face of the town as it used to be.

0 7524 1128 4

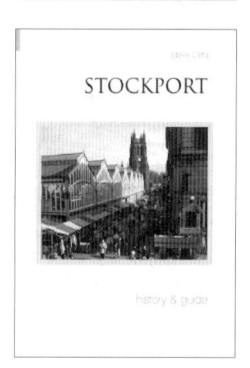

Stockport: History & Guide
STEVE CLIFFE

Originally a border market town above the Mersey with a small medieval castle, Stockport grew into the leading cotton manufacturer of the eighteenth and early nineteenth centuries. This book looks at the evolution of the town to the present day, from Roman activity and the Civil war, through the industrial period, to the arrival of the modern Stockport with the coming of the railway. This book is an essential guide for anyone with an interest in gaining an insight into the proud heritage of this fascinating town.

0 7524 3525 6

If you are interested in purchasing other books published by Tempus, or in case you have difficulty finding any Tempus books in your local bookshop, you can also place orders directly through our website

www.tempus-publishing.com